Malta & Gozo
A Megalithic Journey

Neil McDonald BA (Hons)
Megalithic Publishing
2016

Malta & Gozo - A Megalithic Journey

First Published by Megalithic Publishing 2016

© 2016 Neil McDonald

The rights of Neil McDonald to be identified as author of this work has been asserted in accordance with the Copyright, Design and Patents Act 1988

All rights reserved. No part of this book may be reproduced, stored in or introduced into a retrieval system, or transmitted, in any form or by any other means (electronic, mechanical, photocopying, recording or otherwise) without the written permission of the publisher.

Any person who does any unauthorized act in relation to this publication may be liable to criminal prosecution and civil claims for damages. The book is sold subject to the condition that it shall not, by the way of trade or otherwise, be lent, re-sold, hired out or otherwise circulated, without the publisher's prior consent, in any form or binding cover other than in which it is published, and without similar conditions, including this condition being imposed on the subsequent publications.

ISBN - 978-1-326-59835-8

www.megalithictours.com

Contents

Map of Malta and Gozo, Showing Chapter Division	7
Maltese Timeline	8
Introduction	9
Part 1. A History of Malta and Gozo	12
Chapter 1. Maltese Prehistory	**13**
Formation of a Mediterranean Archipelago	13
Strange Fauna	14
Palaeolithic Controversy	15
Early Neolithic Period	22
Temple Period	25
Desertion	38
Bronze Age	39
Chapter 2. Early Maltese History	**43**
Phoenician Period (Iron Age)	43
Punic Period	47
The Roman Period	49
Chapter 3. Malta's Medieval History	**58**
Byzantine Empire	59
Arab Muslim Period	63
The Maltese Norman Conquest	67
The Swabian House of Hohenstaufen	72
The Capetian House of Anjou	76
The House of Aragon	82

Chapter 4. Knights of St John — 90
From a Brotherhood to an Order — 90
Refuge in Rhodes — 93
Destination Malta — 96
Malta a new island home — 99
The Great Siege — 105
Rising into the Seventeenth Century — 110
Decline into the Eighteenth Century — 117
Loss of Malta and French Occupation — 123
A Modern Order of St John — 128

Chapter 5. The British — 133
Napoleonic Conflict and British Relief — 133
From Protectorate to Colony — 136
Life in Maltese Britain — 141
World War II and the 'Second Great Siege' — 153
Towards Independence — 176

Chapter 6. Malta Today — 180
Malta Today — 180

Part 2. Ancient and Historical sites of Malta and Gozo — 183

Chapter 7. Valletta and Eastern Malta — 184
The National Museum of Archaeology – Valletta — 187
St. John's Co-Cathedral – Valletta — 193
The Presidential Palace & Armory – Valleta — 196
Ħal Saflieni Hypogeum — 201
Kordin Three Temple — 207
Tarxien Temples — 211

Chapter 8. Southern Malta — 223
Birzebbuga Silos & Cisterns — 226
Borġ in-Nadur Temple — 228
Għar Dalam Cave — 231
Ħaġar Qim Temples — 237
Mnajdra Temples — 247
Misqa Tanks — 255
Tas-Silġ Temple — 258
Wied Znuber Dolmen — 264

Chapter 9. Mdina, Rabat and Western Malta — 266
Clapham Junction Cart Ruts & Caves — 270
Domus Romana — 275
St Agatha's Catacombs — 278
St. Paul's Catacombs — 280

Chapter 10. Northern Malta — 284
Buġibba Temple — 287
San Pawl Milqi — 289
Skorba Temple — 294
Ta' Ħaġret Temple — 298
Ta' Hammut — 302
Tal-Qadi Temple — 305
Wied Filep — 308
Xemxija Trail Menhir and Caves — 310
Xemxija Rock-cut tombs — 316

Chapter 11. The Island of Gozo — 322
Museum of Archaeology, Victoria — 325
Ggantija Temples — 328
Qala Menhir — 339
Ta' Ċenċ Dolmen — 341
Xaghra Stone Circle — 344

Epilogue 348

Bibliography 349

Appendix 353
Sites by time period

Malta & Gozo - A Megalithic Journey

Map of Malta and Gozo Showing Chapter Division

Maltese Timeline

Early Neolithic Period	5200 BC
Ghar Dalam	5200 – 4500 BC
Grey Skorba	4500 – 4400 BC
Red Scorba	4400 – 4100 BC
Temple Period	
Żebbuġ	4100 – 3700 BC
Mġarr	3800 – 3600 BC
Ġgantija	3600 – 3200 BC
Saflieni	3300 – 3000 BC
Tarxien	3150 – 2500 BC
Desertion	2500
Bronze Age	
Tarxien Cemetery	2400 – 1500 BC
Borg In-Nadur	1500 – 700 BC
Phoenician	700 – 500 BC
Punic	500 – 218 BC
Roman	218 BC – AD 535
Medieval	
Byzantine	535 - 870
Arab/Muslim	870 - 1090
Norman	1091 - 1194
Hohenstaufen, Swabian	1194 - 1266
Angevin	1266 - 1283
Argonese & Castilian	1283 – 1530
Knights of St John	1530 – 1798
The French	1798 - 1800
The British	1800 - 1964
Independence	21st Sep 1964
Joined the EU	1st May 2004

Introduction

My first visit to the Mediterranean island of Malta was to attend a ten day conference looking at the amazing and unique megalithic temples that stretch across the length of the archipelago. Although I was already used to running tours around the ancient and historical sites of Britain this event was to provide a whole new element to the hobby that had become my full time occupation. This introduction to these overcrowded yet somewhat solitary islands led to a fascination with their rich, complex and layered history that has resulted in many visits over the intervening years.

High on the list of items that make Malta so fascinating are the mysteries, contradictions and controversies that surround their early inhabitants and their constructions. Did human kind arrive on the islands in the Palaeolithic or the Neolithic and if not the earlier date, why not? Although the question is still open the orthodox prehistorical dating systems and points of reference have it that man arrived in the Neolithic, so this book will follow suit to avoid confusion. It is probable, though, that the Neolithic timeline will eventually have to be pushed much further back than the present date of 3,500 BC, especially after the discovery of the monumental Gobeklitepe site in Turkey, that has been dated to 8,000 BC.

The islands have witnessed the growth and disappearance of an extraordinary Neolithic temple society, long before their strategic position became recognised by the many nations who landed, usually as occupying armies. Over the millennia Malta has been ruled by the; Phoenician, Punic, Roman, Arab, Norman, Swabian, Angevin, Argonese, the Knights of St John and the French and British forces, before finally gaining independence in 1964. It is the melting pot of all these diverse cultures that makes Malta the place it is today.

Lying just 50 miles south of Sicily, Malta is much smaller than its neighbour covering an area of only 122 sq miles, with a length of 17 miles and a width of 9 miles. Malta's second island, Gozo sitting less than 4 miles to the northwest is around a third of its size and dimensions and the tiny island of Comino is more or less equidistant between the two. With around 400,000 inhabitants, Malta is by far the most densely populated state in the EU with around 3,250 people per sq mile, compared with only 650 per sq mile in the UK.

The majority of Malta's population is generally located in the south of the island from the capital Valletta down to the area around Birzebbuga and Marsaxlokk on the south coast. Although there are some important towns in the north there are also many open areas and Gozo, in total contrast, appears to be as Malta might have been a hundred years ago. It is during that time that the major growth of population and building took place with no consideration of the positioning of the ancient and historical sites that are located across the whole of the land mass.

The very abundance of remarkable sites in Malta means that it would be impossible to include them all in these pages, so a choice of the very best has been made to represent the various time periods. Equally the road system on the island makes it problematic to include the detailed site directions found in previous 'Megalithic Tours' books, but help and directional hints are provided when possible. The islands have also been divided into 5 chapter sections, to assist with pinpointing the position of sites. It is hoped that this narrowing down of area together with the very size of the island will be helpful as nowhere in Malta is ever that far from your destination.

The purpose of this book is to provide a useful and informative companion on any tour around the island's antiquities. The wonderful year-round sunshine, amazing sea views and plentiful night life that this holiday island, situated in the middle of the Mediterranean are more famous for, will of course be equally welcome during a Maltese adventure.

Part 1

A History of Malta and Gozo

Chapter 1

Maltese Prehistory

Formation of a Mediterranean Archipelago

Earth, our home planet, has been in a constant state of change since its formation some 4 ½ billion years ago. Not only has its climate been in a constant state of flux but its very physical form has altered continually from the smallest transformations to the massive and sometimes devastating movements of the Earth's crust. The area now covered by the Mediterranean is no exception and the Sea is in at least its third period of existence, the first dating back over 222 million years to a time when the movement of the Earth's tectonic plate system led to the creation of a great hollow crater that flooded to form a sea, later named Tethys by the Greeks. During the tertiary period (between 65 and 2.6 million years ago) further earth movement led to Tethys becoming land locked and without an external feed the sea evaporated to form a massive salt desert. As this land mass lay well below sea level it was refilled after massive flooding around 5.6 million years ago and this new sea again evaporated until dry during the following hundreds of thousands of years.

The tranquil and serene Mediterranean Sea that many now derive so much pleasure from was the result of the Zanclean

Flood, a ferocious geological episode the extent of which we can only attempt to imagine. Daniel Garcia-Castellanos, of the Institute of Earth Science Jaume Almera, Barcelona, described how, 5.33 million years ago, tectonic subsidence on the Gibraltar side of the mountains that connected Europe with Africa and erosion caused by water leakage resulted in a flood 'three orders of magnitude larger than the present Amazon river', (Nature (journal) Vol 462, Pg 778, Dec 2009). Garcia-Castellanos explained how the waters of the Atlantic Ocean rushed through the newly formed gap with a 'Column of water going down that slope - several hundred metres deep, and in a channel that would have reached speeds of more than 100km per hour.' The catastrophic gush would have continued for two years forming a sea and cutting the Gibraltar Strait whilst producing the Mediterranean islands, including the Maltese archipelago, in the process. Now with a steady supply of water through the Gibraltar Strait to replace that lost through the constant process of evaporation the Mediterranean Sea was here to stay.

Strange Fauna

The forces of Climatic change continued to affect the Mediterranean and its surrounding land masses until the Pleistocene Period, up to 2 million years ago, when temperatures were swinging massively from warm to extreme cold. It was during this epoch, when much of Europe was experiencing periods of glaciation, that a land bridge was formed between Sicily and Malta due to shifting sea ice to a depth of around 800 ft. The relatively low sea depths between Sicily and Malta of up to 300 ft allowed the causeway to develop providing a passage for animals to the island from the north. Access to the south and Africa was never available due to the deeper seas of over 3,000 ft maintaining a continuous blockage and therefore it can be seen that all the animal life on the island must have arrived from Sicily.

With the passage of many thousands of years the ice melted causing a re-flooding of the land bridge by around 12,000 BC, trapping animals on the Maltese islands and forcing them to compete for a limited food supply. Animal life now had to adapt or become extinct and it is this situation that produced some unusual fauna. The major source of early evidence for this strange wild life was the Ghar Dalam cave in Birzebbugia, (see chapter 8) where excavations provided evidence of such anomalies as giant dormice, tortoises, lizards and swans and pygmy elephants and hippopotamus.

Palaeolithic Controversy
(Before 5200 BC)

The orthodox archaeological theory of Malta's pre-history states that the islands remained unoccupied by humans until the Neolithic Period, around 5200BC. It is evident though that man was travelling around the Mediterranean on boats from as least as long ago as 8000 BC although no remains of these early vessels have been found. The discovery of large pieces of the shiny opaque glass obsidian, which could only have come from the islands of Pantelleria (240 Km west) and Lipari (300 km north) would indicate the presence of such sailors on Malta from before the Neolithic and since the land bridge connecting Malta to Sicily had disappeared after 8000 BC.

This early timeline was pushed further back by two Maltese medical doctors, Anton Mifsud, a Senior consultants and president of the Prehistoric Society of Malta and his son, Simon Mifsud, a senior registrar, in their controversial yet powerfully researched book 'Dossier Malta', that was forwarded by Professor Antony J Frendo, head of Malta Universities Archaeological Department. The argument put forward by Mifsud is that early man would have followed the herds of Red Deer and other sources of food such as, brown bear, red fox and wolf as they headed south across Europe to warmer climes. This would have led them across the, then present, land bridge onto Malta from Sicily, where they had defiantly been present. Remains recovered from the Deer Layer in Malta's Ghar Dalam cave prove that Red Deer were on the island from around 16,000 to 8,000 BC and Mifsud contends that humans would inevitably have followed their prey onto the island and would have therefore been there throughout this period.

As early as 1865 Arturo Issel uncovered the remains of Hippopotamus bones that had been cooked and opened up to reach the marrow and in 1892 John H Cooke recovered a bone from a human hand and some sort of stone tool from the Deer Layer both providing evidence of early man. This population of hunters on such a small island would have had a profound effect on the animal population to the extent that would probably have led to their eventual extinction of many species though overhunting.

Then in 1917 Giuseppi Despott discovered two bull-shaped molar teeth in the Deer Layer, an archaeological horizon at Ghar Dalam (see Ghar Dalam, Chp. 8), that were given the type name 'taurodont' (bull-tooth) by Arthur Keith, who described them as from Neanderthal Man and thus from the Palaeolithic. Keith had also studied 2,250 Neolithic teeth from Malta and found that these were all of a different type than the taurodont variety which had a larger than normal pulp cavity and without roots or a significant waist line. Further teeth were discovered at Ghar Dalam, by Gertrude Caton-Thompson (non-taurodont) in 1924 and Dr J Baldacchino (taurodont), in 1936. Also in 1917 another molar was recovered from the same site by George Sinclair, but the whereabouts of this artefact is unsure.

This evidence of a Palaeolithic presence in Malta was challenged in 1962 by the dentist JJ Mangion, who spoke of finding taurodontism in the modern Maltese population. In fact, the number of modern taurodontal cases were very small and the extent of the condition extremely minor in comparison with the Neanderthal teeth and also some cases of 'fused root syndrome' were confused with the condition. This was all, though, that Professor John D Evans needed to proclaim that Palaeolithic man had never reach Malta and that the earliest human present on the islands was in the Neolithic. This after all had been the basis of his PhD, after graduating from Cambridge in 1949, a qualification that would set him off on an illustrious career as Professor of Prehistoric Archaeology at the University of London. Evans was equally unprepared to accept the stratigraphic evidence in that the taurdontic teeth had been found in the Palaeolithic Deer Layer, strongly indicating that the they were contemporary with this period, but a possibility did exist that the teeth may have been intrusive to the level, having been dropped in or from a later deep burial from a higher level.

In order to answer these questions it was going to be necessary to review tests that had been carried out by the physical anthropologist and Palaeontologist, Kenneth Page Oakley of London's Natural History Museum, who had come to fame in the 1953 having proved that Piltdown Man was a hoax. If these tests, that were completed in 1952, found that the taurdontic teeth were contemporary with the Deer Layer at Ghar Dalam, from where they were recovered, then the matter of the presence of Palaeolithic man in Malta should be proved positively.

Oakley's tests were concerned with the chemical measurement of an artefacts; fluoride, uranium and nitrogen levels, the so called 'FUN analysis'. The premise being, very basically, that after death bone, teeth and antlers etc, would absorb fluoride and uranium from their surroundings at a rate in conjunction with their surroundings and loose nitrogen on the same basis.

The items examined where the three molars from Ghar Dalam; Caton-Thompson's as Ma.1, Despott's as Ma,2 and Baldacchino's as Ma.7 and two teeth from the Hypergeum as Ma. 5 and 6. The results came out as;

Ma.1 – (non-taurodont). Fluoride – 0.2 & 0.3, therefore equal to Red Deer of 0.25 & 0.3, therefore Palaeolithic. Nitrogen – 0.39 & 0.79, the first reading was equal to Hippo molars and therefore of the Palaeolithic, but the second reading is quite higher meaning that the nitrogen result could be said to be inconclusive.

Ma.2 – (taurodent). Flouride is the highest reading of all samples meaning that this tooth is definitely Palaeolithic (up to 0.6). Nitrogen – 1.85 contradicts the fluoride reading but on studying the results page Mifsud makes the serious allegation that this reading had been changed from .8, by overwriting it in heavier ink. If this unproven insinuation is true then the .8 reading would mean that the tooth was Palaeolithic. At the lease the nitrogen result is again unreliable. This sample was tested for Uranium Oxide in 1968 with a result of 13 ppm on a background of 0.1 ppm for living organisms. This result supports the Flouride reading and confirms the tooth as Palaeolithic.

Ma.7 - (taurodent). Nitrogen – 0.44 equal to the Hippo molars from Ghar Dalam of 0.4, thus indicating a Palaeolithic date. This specimen was originally described by Baldaccino as being heavily fossilized before it was stored away somewhere in the Malta museum, but strangely the few visitors that have since seen it report that it is no longer in a fossilized state. This has led to the suggestion by Misfud that the tooth may have been switched at some point although, of course, this could just be the result of a filing error.

Ma.6 – Nitrogen – reading Nil which again indicated that the nitrogen test is unreliable. A later radio-carbon test showed this tooth be of the Tarxien/Neolithic period, which is to be expected from a sample from the Hypogeum.

These results were only published in 1964, a whole decade after the tests were originally carried out and they were in an extremely limited and perhaps misleading form as they concentrated on the unreliable nitrogen results, so it was not until the publication of 'Dossier Malta', that the full story was produced.

During research for his book and Channel 4 series 'Underworld', Graham Hanckock made a request to the Natural History Museum, in London, to examine the Green Book that held all these test results and was informed that the relevant page was missing from the book, removed by some unknown person at an unknown time. Dr Louise Humphrey at the museum also added that she had found the original test results carried out in 1952, containing the results that would have been on the missing page and that the reading of 1.85 for sample Ma.2 was correct, although it is still unclear if the .8 result was also correct. Dr Mifsud, though, stands by his accusation that the document had been tampered with.

Another form of evidence for the presence of Palaeolithic man is the wonderful cave art they produced, which can be found in Europe at such as places as El Castillo and Cave of Altamira, in Spain and Lascaux, Cave of Niaux and Grotte de Cussac in France. Many of these paintings are of animals and amazing designs consisting of hand prints showing incredible sophistication. This art is extremely rare in Europe but are there any to be found in Malta? The answer appears to be a little like the bone results, yes but not in an obvious way. In fact there are three places that would fit the bill to varying extents.

The one place that ancient art can be readily viewed is at the Tarxien South Temple where you can still make out the wonderful carvings of two bulls and a sow chipped out of the rock but this isn't painting and has been dated to the Neolithic to fit with the temple. Then there is the Ghar Hasan cave down on the southern coast in an extremely difficult place to reach on a cliff ledge. Here a group of Italian archaeologists accompanied by the World expert in cave art Emmanuel Anati uncovered a series of around twenty cave paintings from beneath the growth of stalagmites. The art works included depictions of Bovids, deer, elephants and surreal designs like those of handprints all painted in reds, browns and blacks, but they only saw the dim cave light for a very short period and it would take extensive work to uncover them to the extent that they could be seen by visitors. If proof was ever needed of Palaeolithic presence on Malta then the eight photographs of the Ghar Hasan art that Anati, sent to the Museum of Archaeology in 1989, should be it.

The other place where cave art has been witnessed is the Hypogeum, where Trump advised visitors:

'Before descending the stairs to the lower story, visitors should pause to look at the wall opposite them. Dark lines of black paint outline what is apparently intended to be a bull. It is crudely done, and the head and shoulders have not survived. That it is ancient and intentional is shown by the fact that the ochre wash on the wall ceases exactly at the black line.' (Trump, H. David, *Malta: An Archaeological Guide*, Pg 65)

Trump was indicating to potential visitors to the Hypogeum of an ancient depiction of a bison-bull painted on the left wall at the entrance to the 'Holy of Holies', possibly as long ago as the Magdalenian Period, 15,000-10,000 BC. Unfortunately, the necessary preservative low lighting conditions in the hypogeum mean it is difficult to make out the figure and the structures being built to aid the passage of visitors through the site are not helping, also it is only the body that remains as the head and shoulders of this ancient beast have disappeared, or as Dr Mifsud says, removed.

Early Neolithic Period
(5200 - 4100 BC)

Ghar Dalam 5200–4500 BC
Grey Skorba 4500–4400
Red Skorba 4400 – 4100

The Early Neolithic Period was characterized by the beginnings of settlement and the introduction of farming. Although this was a process that had been occurring in mainland Europe at the time it may have been made in some ways necessary in Malta by the extinction of the islands fauna through extensive hunting.

The earliest date that Mankind arrived on the Maltese islands, as covered in the previous section, is by no means certain and the dating of the Early Neolithic Period has been carried out through the testing of pottery shards recovered from the various sites. Although it can never be certain that such evidence dates from the earliest time of construction of these places the dating of pottery shards has nevertheless presented the orthodox dating scale for this time period.

The first of these took its name from the Ghar Dalam cave where fragments were found in the so called 'Cultural or Domestic' excavation layer from a time when the cave was inhabited by settlers, probably from Sicily, as long ago as 5200 BC. Ghar Dalam pottery (Ghar Dalam 5200-4100 BC) was located amongst a great quantity of domestic animal and human remains and stone tools and is described as being a local variety of the 'Impressed Ware' design found in Sicily and other coastal areas of the Mediterranean. The design can be separated into its fine and coarse types, both usually grey and the fine variety had been polished and decorated with repeated impressed lines and incisions. Two recognisable designs often found in the Ghar Dalam deposits were a particular globular jar and small deep bowl. The coarser Ghar Dalam pottery is less well finished and although often grey the colour can also tend towards the brown.

It was discovered during the 1961-3 excavation of the Skorba site, near Mgarr, that the temple had been built on quite an extensive previous construction from the Early Neolithic Period. Below the temples several layers of stratification were found to go down at least 2 metres containing pottery remains. Radiocarbon dating of charcoal showed that the fragments were from the already recognised Ghar Dalam Period but included two new varieties that were named after the site, thus creating two further time periods, (Grey Skorba 4500–4400 BC and Red Skorba 4400–4100 BC).

Both forms of Skorba pottery have distinctive white speckles throughout as a result of the construction and firing process whilst the design styles can be seen to progress from the Ghar Dalam. Polished open bowls and dippers are common designs often with rounded horizontal lug handles with dimples to each end, as is a characteristic ladle with a broad handle and V shaped end. It is the later Red Skorba that shows a distinctive red slip that has often been recorded in Sicily and on main land Italy but the Skorba pottery is characterized again by the white speckles and the continuation of local Maltese design.

Although much of the early building at Skorba is hidden beneath the later temples the site proved to be invaluable in the study of the time of the first farming settlers in Malta. Amongst the plethora of pottery to be found in two rooms to the east of the main site were goat sculls and figurines suggesting the presence of an early religious shrine. A further somewhat unexpected discovery was that apart from the lowermost stone brick layer of the walls to these Neolithic rooms, which would have acted as footings, the remainder of the walls were constructed from mud brick, made from the local Blue Clay, raising the question of why such building materials were utilized on an island with so much easily fashioned stone. The floors to these buildings were of solid bedrock.

From the various remains found in the Neolithic sites a basic profile can be suggested of the lives of these early Maltese farmers. It is clear that they practiced mixed farming as the bones of domesticated animals were found amongst the remains of various crops such as wheat and barley. These cereals would have been ground into flour with the use of stone saddle querns carved from coralline limestone. Spindle whorls were also uncovered, mainly from the Red Skorba Period, indicating the spinning of textiles and so the manufacture of fabrics. This indicates the production of clothing that could have been coloured using natural dyes. To accompany these were various forms of jewellery such as perforated shells and carved and decorated stone pendants finished off with the use of pumice. It is probable that some hunting continued into the Neolithic as many globigerina limestone rocks, carved into lemon shapes around 5 cm long and ideal for sling shot have been located. Tools for the shaping of these and other implements have been uncovered including stone flints and blades of up to 4 cm in length. A small quantity of stone axe heads, many imported from foreign sources were found together with smaller versions of around 3 cm long that were probably used for decoration or religious purposes. From the existence of these artefacts and the similarity of some pottery designs it would seem that constant contact and interaction would have been maintained with Sicily.

Temple Period
(4100-2500 BC)

Zebbug 4100 – 3700 BC - Mgarr 3800 – 3600 BC
Ggantija 3600 – 3200 BC - Saflieni 3300 – 3000 BC
Tarxien 3150 – 2500 BC

The dating of Malta's magnificent temples is one of conjecture and a much earlier timeline than the one suggested by present orthodoxy may one day be produced for their construction. The current archaeological theory has it that around 3,500 BC the first building of stone structures took place in Europe, although the recent dating of the huge Gobeklitepe site in Turkey, to 8,000 BC, effectively shifts this time horizon back 5,500 years. The dating of the Maltese Neolithic buildings was carried out with the original time period in mind and supported by a very few radio-carbon dating results. This method only tests organic material that could have been presented to the site at a much later date than their construction.

For the purposes of this book and without a definite dating for a probably earlier time scale it is necessary to follow the present orthodox dating scales, always bearing in mind, though, that the temples could have been built much further back in antiquity than discussed here.

Nevertheless, transition into the Temple Period of Malta's Neolithic Age appears to have been seamless in regard to the island's resident farmers and agricultural practices. The date of 4100 BC given to the start of this period appears somewhat misleading as the earliest recorded temple construction was not until around 3500 BC. This apparent 600 year discrepancy is accounted for by the discovery of rock cut tombs around the islands dating back as far as 4100 BC and used continually until 2500 BC. This provides evidence of either skills development in the resident population or the influx of a new immigrant populace as this innovative form of burial practice was present throughout the Mediterranean landmasses.

Rock cut tombs initially consisted of a vertical, or in some cases diagonal, shaft leading down into the sheer rock and culminating in an oval shaped burial chamber with a flat lower surface and the longest elevation lying horizontal. The chambers were used for multiple burials with any skeletal remains already present being moved to one side to make room for the next. In some cases bones would be arranged by type with long bones piled together and skulls collected separately, much in the way as was done in later British chambered tombs. The bodies would then have often received a thin covering of red ochre which remained present after the burial sites were excavated in the form of red tainted soil.

Rock Cut tomb at Xemxija

Also found in the tombs were the remains of grave goods such as pottery bowls, axe heads and figurines. After burials the tombs would be sealed with removable rock slabs, that in some cases would be carved to fit around the site entrance and which could be rolled out of the way to reopen the tomb when further burial was needed. Occasionally two or three steps were carved into the side of the entrance shaft to help with access. With time more chambers were added to many tombs, no doubt to provide extra burial space for a larger local population and in Xemxija the tombs have two, three and in one case five separate and adjoining chambers.

The architectural scene on the Maltese islands took a fundamental, astonishing and somewhat unexplained leap around 3500 BC with the building of the first above ground temples, an achievement that saw the induction of a religious way of life that was to last 1,000 years. How the builders of these monuments moved the massive stone slabs cannot be explained today through comparison with any other society as nowhere else in the world were such free standing stone buildings being erected. The pyramids of Egypt came much later, towards the end of the Maltese Temple Period and in Britain we were mainly constructing the earliest of the stone circles.

An answer to the riddle of the derivation of the stone temples may possibly be found in the design of the rock cut tombs. The shape of these burial chambers suggests a precursor to the later above ground temples providing a suggestion as to how a farming community could suddenly begin building temples of such sophistication and complexity of design and engineering. The practice of mirroring below ground structures in buildings built on the surface appears to have been eventually reversed in the elaborate carvings of the subterranean Hal Salflieni, Hypogeum where features such as corbelled ceilings and trillathons were expertly carved into the very rock as decorative featuring. Whilst similarities in design exist between rock cut tombs and the temples, this can only suggest at some sort of a connection between the architects of these ancient structures but it goes nowhere near to providing a decisive answer to the sudden arrival of the stone temples of Malta and this remains one of the greatest mysteries of the megalithic world.

Far from providing any solution to this Neolithic riddle a closer look at the positioning and orientation of the temples only confounds the situation as there appears to be no apparent consistency across the islands. The temples seem to be spaced out randomly across the landmass with no particular plan to their location and whether they were situated to serve a local populace is not known due to the near total absence of dwelling remains from the period. When considering the religious practices of an ancient people it is all too easy to place on them behaviours of our own but it is entirely possible that the temples did not serve as local churches and could, for example, have been occupied by a priestly class providing blessings for seafarers. The directionality of Western Christian buildings provides some insight into the associated belief system as they have the altar to the east towards the rising sun and mosques are orientated to qibla, the Keeba stone in Mecca whereas the direction of most of the Malta temples does not appear to be overly significant. The majority of openings look out through the arc from southwest to southeast although one of the Mnajdra temples faces east and a major opening at Hagar Qim looks north.

So what evidence can we work from in order to build up some sort of a picture of these most enigmatic of ancient folk? Well most importantly we have the physical structures that they created and which amazingly still stand for us to explore after more than five millennia, the temples themselves. The individual buildings do differ greatly in detail but they all appear to have been constructed from one overall architectural plan.

Haġar Qim Temple Façade – Forecourt, Benches & Orthostats

Firstly the solid rocky ground of the building site had to be levelled and a forecourt, usually oval in shape, was created with stone terracing to the boundaries when required. This area was probably for the gathering of people with temple business and a few stone benches appear to have been built into the edges of some buildings. The temple façades are still striking even today and would have been an awe-inspiring sight to any ancient people experiencing a freestanding building for the first time. The ground layer of this external front elevation was constructed with large megalithic blocks, or orthostats, laid face on and with larger blocks to either end. Further orthostats would be attached to these and placed alternatively side then edge on to form the outer edge of the building as it curved its way around to the rear. This alternate placing of stone blocks had the effect of tying the walls together thus providing the great strength required to hold the whole building in place without the use of mortar. The large gap between the external and internal walls was filled with rubble further strengthening the overall structure.

Entrance and passage to inner Apse at Tarxien Temple

Above the lower orthostats further megaliths were laid in various horizontal levels to provide the required height of the building and a base for any roof. A front entrance was formed by placing two orthostats edge on to the facia with a gap between them and with a flat lintel stone connecting them by laying it across the top to form a Stonehenge-like trilithon (three stones).

This doorway leads through a short passage lined with further roofed trilithons and floored in stone paving that takes you through the thickness of the outer and inner walls. This in turn leads to an open inner space that may be seen as a continuation of the passageway with curved 'D' shaped rooms to each side known as apses. The floor covering in this interior area could again be of stone but it is much more likely to be 'torba' a form of toughened plaster made from ground globigerina limestone laid over a rubble underpinning and treated to repeated whetting and pounding until it turned solid and could be polished. The apses were probably built open plan but many were later partitioned off with orthostat walls some with trilithon entrances and others with so called 'portholes', or large megaliths with square holes cut through to provide access. These portholes often had inner chamfered edges to allow either the removed stone or a wooden board to be replaced and tied shut from within, we are not sure which. Both Globigerina and Coralline limestone were used throughout the temples for both internal and external walls, the former being far more easily shaped. In some cases apse walls are created in the same manner as externally with upstanding orthostats below horizontal layers of megaliths but in some cases the whole wall was formed out of smaller blocks of the more durable Coralline.

Inner Apse showing the beggings of roof corbelling and possible Oricle Hole at *Haġar Qim Temple*

The simplest form of temple is the trefoil design that includes a third apse opposite the doorway to produce the shape of an Ace of Spades playing card. In most cases though, an additional passageway was created in the position of the third apse leading through to another forecourt and two further apses and it is this process of extension from the original trefoil design that provides the individual character and shape of each temple. Further chambers built into the thickness of the temple walls utilising similar porthole entrances and additional passageways leading from the middle of apse walls with further attached apses resulted in the development of some quite complicated and extensive designs.

As suggested above, entrances and inner passageways were roofed with stone lintels and on excavation fragments of internal plastering found from the Temple Period indicated that the apse areas were also roofed. Further evidence of roofing was derived from the various small temple models also discovered during excavation but it was not clear from these what roofing material was used. The upper portions of some apse walls appear to overhang slightly towards the centre of the space in a way that would indicate the beginnings of a corbelled roof, a process that may have been finished off in vaulted arch, or more likely topped off with a large flat capstone. Other walls though do not appear to have been sturdy enough to hold stone slabs so it is possible that some temple apses were covered with wooden beams, a theory that is supported by the discovery of charcoal remains within some walls.

Considering their antiquity the quality of workmanship throughout the temples is incredible and that is nowhere more apparent than their interior design. Beginning with simple pitted holes, probably created with a rotary bow drill and covering whole megalithic slabs, through simple and then more elaborate spirals with thorn offshoots, to multiple animals.

There are various features included in temple design that tend to repeat to varying degrees including the presence of one huge megalith that stands out over the height of the rest of the building to the rear. Also of interest are the so called 'oracle holes', small apertures cut through an apse wall, sometimes with an external area that would appear to be for the use of visitors awaiting the fruits of priestly divination. The major recurring aspects of temple furniture are, though, the altars mainly found in the style of trilithons with the upper lintel possibly used as the ceremonial area, although some would appear to be too high for this purpose. There are also smaller free standing pillar altars some with the fine elaborate pit carved decoration. The existence of so many altars would appear to provide overwhelming evidence that these building are in fact for religious purposes and not, for example, schools but it is difficult to dig down much further into any system of belief. The presence of apparent tethering holes at the entrance of some temples, together with the discovery of piles of domestic animal bones and long flint knives next to some altars, would strongly suggest animal sacrifice. It is also clear that fire played some sort of role within the temples whether just for illumination in an otherwise dark environment or for ceremonial purposes it is uncertain. Heat from fire would also have found a use in warming the contents of a huge stone cauldron, found in pieces during excavation and meticulously reconstructed, whatever those ingredients would have been.

With regard to the character of the religious belief system of our temple people much speculation has been derived from comparing the very shape of a basic temple with the many 'Fat Lady Statues', uncovered. These figures, ranging in size from a few centimetres to one which would have stood up to nearly three metres tall, must have had some great significance to temple activities but, again, details are absent. It is tempting to look on these figures as evidence of a goddess culture but in fact the sex of the statues is somewhat ambiguous and more suggestive of hermaphroditism. If this were the case it would be indicative of a dualistic philosophy whereby the opposites that we all experience in this Earthly construct, up/down, in/out, black/white, male/female have been overcome in the deity. But there were many statues of different sizes and types found within the temples and how these fit into the picture is not clear but these will be considered in the sections covering the individual temples.

So we have a bizarrely sophisticated temple culture appearing apparently with no prelude society but what of life outside the temples? Logic would suggest that the islands religion would serve an equally high civilization with the high population required to build and maintain it. History has shown us that it is normal for such an advanced religious culture to be accompanied by a hierarchical structure with well defined rulers and associated opulence remaining in other buildings, jewellery and graves, but on Malta there is none of this. Wars would also be expected at this level of advancement but again there is absolutely nothing to indicate any sort of general conflict. Where such a population lived is a mystery and in fact amazingly only three possible homes have been located, built from mud brick and sometimes with torba flooring although these may have been constructed before the temples. It is possible that the population built their homes from mud brick and that these consequently disintegrated in time, but why would this material be used on an island with a plentiful supply of easy workable stone? It could not be said that they didn't have the required knowledge of masonry as the presence of the temples would prove otherwise. There is evidence of a small amount of trade with the surrounding islands, in the form of obsidian, flint, red ochre etc but this would not appear to be of the extent expected.

The process of subdividing a time period in respect to its developing and changing pottery styles continues through the

Early Neolithic into the Temple Period where the timeline is broken down as follows;

Zebbug (4100–3700 BC)
Mgarr (3800–3600 BC)
Ggantija (3600–3200 BC)
Saflieni (3300–3000 BC)
Tarxien (3150–2500 BC)

Around the commencement of the Zebbug period pottery showed a definite shift in style probably resulting from ideas brought over to the islands from Sicily. Bowls and pear shaped jars had an original, extra-rugged appearance and the speckled finish of the Skorba designs has gone whilst random striping, some in red, together with stylized human stick figures were new. From this point forward pottery production became steadily more refined and durable through the remaining Temple Period and whilst decorative features changed there were no great jumps in style. Specialists in the field have recorded these changes as they developed but for our purposes the resulting time period classifications are somewhat arbitrary and out of the range of this book.

Throughout the Temple Period an unusually highly advanced people existed on the islands of Malta and Gozo apparently centred around a number of temples of enigmatically sophisticated design and engineering. Where these people came from and how they came upon such highly developed ideas and capabilities is a mystery to us today but the end of this period in Maltese prehistory is equally ambiguous.

The Desertion
(2500 BC)

Until a moment in time around 2500 BC life in the temples of Malta appears to have continued as it had for 1,000 years and then suddenly and apparently abruptly the island population disappeared. No reason for this has even been found and it is probable that this megalithic mystery will never be solved.

If this sudden desertion had been due to a natural disaster then either a layer of dust would have been discovered during excavation or the temples themselves would have been ruined but neither of these circumstances occurred. As no human dwellings have remained on the islands, overpopulation and the resulting excess burden on resources would appear unlikely. The lack of skeletal damage or the location of weapons from the temple period would indicate that both war and foreign invasion can be ruled out. It is possible that the islanders fell victim of an infectious disease, such as a form of the plague, but evidence of this would not show itself today so this can neither be ruled in or out.

Another ancient community that was extremely advanced for its time and location was the Neolithic settlement of Skara Brae on the Scottish island of Orkney, thought to originate around 3200 BC. Strangely the megalithic stone builders who constructed this sophisticated group of dwellings also deserted them around 2500 BC, the same date given for the abandonment of Malta. Again the reasons for leaving Orkney have never been agreed on and remain a mystery. Curiously 2500/2600 BC is also around the time given for the beginnings of construction of the earliest Egyptian pyramids.

Bronze Age
(2500/2000-700 BC)

Tarxien Cemetery 2400-1500 BC
Borġ in-Nadur 1500-700 BC
Baħrija 900-700 BC

After the Temple People abandoned Malta and Gozo the islands remained uninhabited until some point before 2000 BC when settlers from Sicily, Italy and further afield began arriving. This influx began slowly with limited settlement as indicated by the small amount of burials found from the earliest period of the Bronze Age. An excavated level in the southern Tarxien temple did reveal though, an important burial area of many cremation pots that became known as the Tarxien Cemetery and which gave its name to the period. Further findings from this phase were located in a low layer beneath Borġ in-Nadur, where a whole Bronze Age village had been built near the much older temple. Above this early layer were further strata from the later 'Borġ in-Nadur' phase indicating continuing and much increased occupation of the area.

The few huts excavated here were characterised by, torba flooring and low stone wall footings although it is not certain what material would have been used for the upper portion of the walls, stone or mud brick or even wattle and daub. The roofs would probably have been of wooden cross branches with a thatch type covering and each hut appeared to have similar fixtures and fittings including a hearth and a grain quern. The whole area of the settlement was up to four hectares and as the houses were built in close proximity it would have been home for several hundred people. An increase in the island's population at this time may have placed some pressure on the availability of accommodation as the finding of Bronze Age deposits in previously deserted cave dwellings would indicate re-inhabitation.

The third phase of Malta's Bronze Age is named after Baħrija in the north of the island, the opposite end to Borġ in-Nadur, in the south near Birżebbuġa. This large peninsula held many pottery shards from the second and third phase spread across its plateau area as well as many storage cavities cut into the rock. These 'silos' or 'cistern tanks' that were a common feature of the later Bronze Age were probably used to store grain for local consumption or even export.

Common artefacts uncovered in excavation of settlements of the Bronze Age included jewellery, clay figures and bronze articles such as needles, rings and bracelets. Stone spindle whorls and loom weights are evidence of textile manufacturing, whilst other bronze items such as axes and daggers could have been used as decorative items or tools and, of course weapons. Although no sign remains of warring or conflict many, but not all, of the settlements had some defensive elements, particularly large walls, built to protect vulnerable areas. This is the first time that such fortification had been thought necessary on Malta and it was possibly a reflection of the introduction of more effective metal weapons to the island.

In general Bronze Age life on Malta didn't seem to be much different than for the Temple People, although these new settlers bringing metal to the island for the first time, did not appear to have any connection with the previous population.

The island's hot climate and limited natural resources would to a great extent dictate how people lived but it appears that farming of crops and animals was wide spread and the proximity to the sea would mean an ever plentiful supply of fish. It is thought that very little metal production took place on the island so the finding of so many bronze artefacts would most likely be from a mixture of trade and people travelling to and from the nearby mainland.

Nothing emphasizes the difference between the Temple Period and Bronze Age culture more than the pottery styles of the two epochs, the newer being much more substantial, coarser and thicker. It is widely held that the two styles could not have derived from the same people. A whole range of new innovative designs were introduced like twin connected bowls, duck shaped jugs with rounded bases and large robust double handled carrying pitchers all decorated with attractive chevrons, criss-cross and multiple line designs.

Burial customs had also changed from the Temple Period practice of lying corpses out in rock cut tombs to that of cremation and placing the burned remains in burial urns together with selected grave foods, as we saw in the Tarxien Cemetery. Whilst this process would have been wide spread it was in the island's Bronze Age that dolmens were constructed and around a dozen of these burial chambers have been located across Malta and Gozo. Structures like dolmen can be found around Europe, Indian and Africa indicating that travel must have been widespread at this time. They consisted of a huge cap stone supported by upright megaliths in order to form an internal chamber. This stone frame would have been covered with large curb-stones and then possibly with a layer of soil with the resulting appearance of an earthen mound. In

Britain, dolmen and long-barrows are often considered to be sacred places akin to temples in their own right where it is thought religious ceremonies would take place that included the buried ancestors.

Pentre Ifan Dolman, South Wales

With the people of the temples long gone a whole new society had developed ushering in Malta's Bronze Age and a way of life that developed organically to last over 1,500 years until external forces would finally deliver that inevitable commodity, change.

Chapter 2

Early Maltese History

Phoenician Period
(700 – 500 BC & Iron Age)

Around 3000 BC the people that became known as the Phoenicians occupied a large part of the massive ancient Near Eastern Levant that stretched inland from the eastern shores of the Mediterranean and was surrounded by the Arabian Desert to the south, Mesopotamia to the east and the Taurus Mountains to the north. This was the Biblical Land of Canaan and the Phoenicians knew themselves as the Canaanites, a people with important ancestry, the original tribal leader 'Canaan' being the Grandson of Noah. It was the Greeks who first named them Phoenicians, or 'Phoinikes', the 'purple people', after the purple dye from the Murex snail that stained the fabrics they used to trade in and quite often stained the workers skin as well. Another possible translation of Phoinikes is red and this could have come from a connection with the glowing complexion of these ruddy sea tanned mariners.

By 1200 BC incoming tribes and general unrest in the Levant had forced the Phoenicians onto the east coast of the Mediterranean where they formed independent city states along the coastal strip of today's Lebanon, north to Arwad in Syria and south to Israel's Mount Carmel. The major Phoenician cities included Biruta (Beirut), Byblos, Hazor, Sarepta and Sidon with the peninsular/island state of Tyre being the principle centre. Having a desire to trade externally but being severely restricted to the east by the Lebanon Mountain range and hostile forces beyond, the Phoenicians headed west out to sea, building trading routes throughout the Mediterranean and beyond. Their insatiable desire to travel took them past the Pillars of Hercules, or the Rock of Gibraltar and out into the open Atlantic, north to Britain as far as Cornwall and it is suggested, further north again up the western 'megalithic' fringe of England, Wales and on to the Scottish islands.

So the Phoenicians set out to sea in their huge boats originally made from the cedar and cypress trees so plentiful in the Lebanon. They would have followed the natural sea currents in an anti-clockwise direction, hugging the coast where possible but avoiding the sandbanks and shallow waters of the infamous Syrtis off the coasts of Libya and Tunisia. Trade was plentiful and the Phoenicians, thriving, began to plant settlements along their sea routes, a process that led to mass colonization along the Mediterranean coast, mainly in North Africa and Spain with Carthage as the principle western city. As in the Lebanon, these cities remained independent and were probably administered by the leading trading families within but were not part of a larger centralized Phoenician state.

At some point around 700 BC Phoenician traders began to put down roots in Malta, naming it Maleth (safe haven), where, strangely shunning their usual choice of a coastal location, they took up residence high on the rocky hilltop plateau of Mdina. As any tourist to Malta's ancient capital soon discovers the views from Mdina, across the island and out over the Mediterranean are amazing. These panoramic sea views would have provided the Phoenician colonists with just the early warning of any encroaching enemy that they would have needed. Down on the south east coast the huge natural harbour of Marsaxlokk Bay was chosen as a secure place to land on the island, ideally situated as it is to take ships on the westward trading route from the Lebanon. Many of the coves here provided shallow sandy beaches where boats could run aground at this time before stone harbour quays had been introduced. Tas-Silġ hill overlooking Marsaxlokk Bay also became an important place to the Phoenicians who adopted the site of a Tarxien Period temple there converting it into a 'Temple of Astarte', or Ashtart their chief Goddess. From this highpoint the Goddess could overlook Marsaxlokk Bay and give her blessing to the ships heading out on their long sea journeys of trade.

The predominance of rock cut tombs from this period found around Mdina and surrounding areas indicates that this became the major Phoenician settlement on the island. Other such burial places were located scattered around both Malta and Gozo suggesting the development of much additional dwelling. It is thought that whilst mixing and trading, where possible, with the indigenous Bronze Age population it was only a matter of time until the newcomers outnumbered them to become the dominant Maltese race. Moving towards 600 BC some urgency amongst western Phoenician colonies became apparent in response to Greek expansion resulting in the greater political and military presence of Carthage. An integral response to these developments seems to have been the shifting of Maltese allegiance from Tyre in the east to Carthage although it is probable that Malta and Gozo remained only minor colonial outposts with the primary role of a safe stopping-off point for shipping.

From the beginnings of the 7th Century the Phoenician colonists had a tremendous effect on the Maltese islands but produced few long lasting architectural remains. Malta would have had little in the way of forestry at the time so dwellings from the period would probably have been built of wood transported by ship from the eastern shores of the Mediterranean and these would have long since perished. The rock cut tombs used by the Phoenicians were found to contain much pottery of the period together with stone figures and other ornamental ware of ivory and precious metals, including Egyptian gold.

As for religious buildings, the temple at Tas-Silġ, dedicated to Astarte is by far the most predominant, but a question still remains about the chief God Baal Hammond, the consort of the Goddess. It is highly probable that Baal would have been venerated by the Phoenicians through ceremonies that may have included 'molk' or child sacrifice although the less appalling 'molk omor' or animal sacrifice would have also been a possibility.

But these intrepid seafarers did initiate some crucially important developments to the islands such as smelted metals and therefore the Iron Age and writing through the introduction of the Phoenician Alphabet. This so called proto-Canaanite script, which was spread throughout the Mediterranean by Phoenician merchants, was the forerunner of the Greek alphabet and therefore all western languages.

Punic Period
(500 – 218 BC)

As far as the islands of Malta and Gozo were concerned the move into the Punic Period would have been unnoticeable with no influx of new populations, in fact the Punics were the exact same people as the Phoenicians that had inhabited the islands for the previous two centuries. This was more of a time where allegiances shifted; it was a time of great warring and power struggles between the mighty nations of Persia, Greece, Phoenicia and Rome.

As already eluded to in the previous section the Phoenician alliance in the western Mediterranean had felt a need to increase its military strength in reaction to Greek expansion and this led to the major Western Phoenician city of Carthage growing in administrative importance. With eastern Phoenicia, centred on the city of Tyre, being increasingly influenced by Persia, the development of Carthaginian power was exacerbated until it became the supreme Phoenician authority in the western Mediterranean. It is this new realm with Carthage as its capital that the Romans named Punic and this title that stuck, although the greater domain was also known as Carthage.

From the beginnings of the Punic Period the two powers of Rome and Carthage grew in strength but they were relatively evenly matched and in 509 BC, the year of the foundation of the Roman Republic, they signed a treaty of non-aggression. Life on Malta though, remained pretty much as it had been with mixed farming that included wheat, barley, figs, olives for oil, vines for wine and flax for linen. Trading of the fruits of this agricultural activity along with textiles continued to play a vital role for these maritime merchants.

The political situation in the region had been developing as Rome had increased its military and political control along the Italian peninsula and it very much wanted to add the Greek-occupied island of Sicily to its realm of influence. A turn of events in the Sicilian town of Messana brought Rome and Carthage into conflict when Agathocles, the ruler of Syracuse, hired mercenaries to attack and take the town. Messana town leaders called to Carthage for assistance but when the Punic armies arrived they then called for the help of Rome who also obliged causing major conflict between the two regional powers that led to the 'First Punic War' (264-241 BC).

As is so often the case in times of war the increase in conflict in the Mediterranean saw an exponential increase in trade and in this case it was accompanied by an increase in population, as indicated by the quantity of burials found on both Malta and Gozo. It was also at this time that further large centres of population grew up around the ends of the Grand Harbour on Malta and in Gozo's Rabat. The growth of the populace could to some extent have been a result of the proximity of Sicily and the need to garrison forces near enough to be available when needed whilst remaining over the sea at a safe distance. This grown Punic state thus became Malta's first controlling foreign power and with this came the inevitable taxes with Carthage introducing tithes based on the national yearly harvest that would mainly be used to pay for the war.

Hostilities did reach Maltese soil though in 255 BC when Roman forces, concerned about its strategic position in relation to Sicily, landed on the island and ransacked the countryside leaving no crops that could have been used to sustain Punic troops. With the end of the First Punic war conflict continued to affect the day to day existence of the Maltese people but with the arrival of the second major conflict events were to be brought nearer to home.

The Roman Period
(218 BC - 330 AD)

Beginning in 264 BC, the first Punic War was fought between Rome and the Carthagian forces over Sicily, Malta's neighbouring island and when hostilities ceased in 241 BC the majority of Sicily had become a province of Rome. Sardinia and Corsica, the other two larger Mediterranean islands off the coast of Italy were also annexed by the Roman Republic in 238 BC and by this time the strategic position of Malta was bringing it under increasing focus. In response to this threat, Carthage, having lost much territory, increased its military presence in Malta and by the outbreak of the Second Punic War (218 - 201 BC) they had installed a garrison of around 2,000 troops.

Carthage used the years after the First Punic War to rebuild its strength and to gain territory along the Mediterranean Iberian coast and it was the taking of the Spanish town of Saguntum (today Sagunto, near Valencia), by Hannibal, after a long siege in 219 BC, which led to the Second Punic War. When Carthage refused demands to withdraw from Saguntum, Rome declared war with the assessment that its strategic maritime advantage would ensure a speedy victory against the Punic forces. Their judgment though did not take into consideration Hannibal's thorough determination that led to one of histories most famous acts of military resolve. Understanding that the odds of any attack by sea would by seriously stacked against him he set out towards Rome overland with around 50,000 troops, 9,000 cavalry and a company of 37 war-elephants. This incredible journey took Hannibal from Spain, through France (Gaul), over the Alps and onto the plains of Italy's Po River, losing much of his forces along the way. Arriving in Italy Hannibal fought a lengthy campaign, initially with a large amount of success, but eventually defeated he returned to Carthage in 203 BC. This great general will always be remembered for his immense tenacity and the Second Punic War is often known as the 'Hannibalic War', (General Hannibal Barca 247 – 182 BC, meaning 'mercy of Baal', in Phoenician)

With the taking of Saguntum by the Carthaginians and the consequential declaration of war Rome decided that Malta's strategic position, to the south of Sicily, proposed an unnecessary threat and landed on the island in 218 BC. Strangely, even though Malta had prepared defences against invasion and was protected by a 2,000 strong Punic defence force, it gave in without a fight and Malta became part of the Sicilian Province of the Roman Republic.

For the first two centuries under Rome, Malta and Gozo were administered as a 'civitas', or a centre of population with a greater than average proportion of local independence. The major reason for this local congress was the creation and maintenance of records under the leadership of a Praetor for the purpose of the payment of taxes. In the case of most of the Sicilian territories these were calculated on the yield of the yearly harvest, which being a relatively reasonable system of levying duties allowed the islands a time of quiet prosperity. Local minting of coinage was permitted on the islands although only copper production was allowed and these could not be used for the payment of taxes as duties paid in cash had to be in silver or gold. Even though this ensured that only real wealth would be sent to the central power in Rome, a study of Malta's coins uncovered during excavation showed increasing denomination indicating an amount of inflation and a growing standard of living amongst the general population.

As a further tax on local labour, the civitas would also have been given quotas for the construction, furnishing and crewing of ships to be supplied to central Rome for use in war and trade. Maritime business would have provided a minor tax loophole for the Maltese as only land production would have been eligible so revenues resulting from trade carried out from ships would have been exempt. Although sea trade was a highly significant activity for the Maltese islands being situated as they are on shipping trade routes, the activity would have been fraught with danger from the great number of pirates that plagued the Mediterranean and who used Malta as their winter domicile, until 'Pompey the Great' put a definite end to piracy in 67 BC.

With the final battle of the Third Punic War (149 - 146 BC) and the ultimate destruction of the city of Carthage, Malta lost any remaining military strategic importance that it had held. Thus its relationship with Rome reduced in significance and local priorities would be more or less limited to the administration of public utilities and works, the taking of a five yearly census and tax collection.

The central authorities did not attempt to impinge on Malta's local culture and the Punic language continued to be used except for official documents which were completed in Latin. The ancient religions dating back through the Phoenicians also continued well into Roman times whilst the practice of veneration of the various Gods and Goddesses would have begun to incorporate their equivalent deities from the belief systems of Greece, Egypt and Rome and the funerary practices of inhumation in rock cut tombs and cremation both continued. Industry also carried on much as it had before Roman times with the production of textiles being of great importance as was olive oil and the farming of grain and livestock, probably consisting mainly of sheep and goats. As with any islands of their size, fishing and sea produce would always have been significant, if only for local consumption.

During the first century BC the Republic was experiencing civil war and severe unrest within its boundaries, so serious that it could have brought an end to Rome. As the heir to Julius Caesar, who was assassinated in 44 BC (the ides of March), Gaius Octavian brought together a divided state when in 27 BC the Senate made him Princeps, or 'first citizen' with the power of proconsular imperium 'sovereign authority over the state' and changed his name to Augustus. Thus the days of the Republic were over and the Roman Empire was born in a highly successful move that ushered in an era of two centuries of relative harmony that became known as 'Pax Romana', or the time of Roman Peace.

The political manoeuvres in Rome had some minor effects in the way that Malta was administered stemming mainly from the change of municipal status from civitas to that of stipendior. The major adjustment was in the way that tax was calculated from the taking of a proportion of the yearly harvest to a fixed rate, a less favourable situation financially for Malta especially in years of poor crop yields. Also the right to mint coins was removed from the Sicilian provinces and this would have had the effect of reducing independence and increasing control of Malta and Gozo from the central government in Rome

Trade and industry would have continued much in the same way as it had under the Republic and the islands would have remained quite prosperous. Much of the activity would have centred on the two major cities of Gaulos on Gozo and Melite, or Melita, on Malta, with smaller population areas growing up like the one at the head of the Grand Harbour with direct access across to the now friendly Sicily. Many rural villas would have also been spread around the countryside, these elaborate homes of the wealthy fell mainly into the two categories of residential and rustic. The residential homes were built for opulent comfort with up to 20 rooms including heated flooring systems running from furnaces that would have also served the typical Roman bathing hot rooms (caldarium), warm rooms (tepidarium) and cold baths (frigidarium). The centrepiece of the properties would have been the pillared courtyard (peristyle), surrounded by a veranda and corridor (atrium) with rooms off maybe with highly coloured mosaic flooring. The 'Villae Rustica' would have been similar, if maybe not so lavish, they were homes and places of production combined, usually containing olive oil press rooms and the other machinery required for producing this and other products. It is likely that the villas would have been decorated with colourful frescos and elaborately carved busts and statues, some of which have survived and can be found in the island's museums.

The principal Roman city of Melite grew out of the earlier Punic town covering the landmass that is now Mdina with much of Rabat although today there is very little remaining. The Romans would have appreciated the strategic elevated position of the existing town with its views around much of the island and out to sea providing early warning of any encroaching danger and a high steep cliff to discourage invasion. To cover the remaining, more vulnerable southern aspect of the town, the Romans had a deep ditch dug to provide some level of tactical protection. Just beyond this boundary ditch and so outside the town limits, which would have been a Roman legal requirement, many rock cut burial tombs dating back through Phoenician times had been joined together to form huge complexes of catacombs. These would have been in continual use through Roman and into Christian times. Today these are known as St Paul's and St Agatha's Catacombs that can still be visited. Archaeological digs have revealed that Melite was not built to any grid design as is often the case with Roman cities, but would have grown organically following the natural geographic contours of the land, whilst adding to the buildings already present. The best preserved Roman building on Malta, the Roman Domvs, stands outside the Mdina gates and has been converted into an interesting museum. It would have stood amongst other homes of the period some of which were uncovered temporarily by a dig in 1881. Gaulos, the major Roman town on Gozo grew up in much the same way as its Maltese counterpart, out of the existing Punic centre that is now the town of Rabat, or Victoria. Again there is no discernable street plan but various artefacts can still be seen from the period in the Gozo Archaeological Museum and the Folklore museum both in the Old Town.

As the years and decades rolled by the prevailing culture of the Maltese islands would have been increasingly Romanized particularly for the upper echelons of society; the use of Latin becoming more widespread, again amongst the more wealthy citizens, although the Punic language remained in general usage and religious practises probably moved further towards the use of the Roman pantheon with the site at Tas-Silg remaining important.

Rome eventually entered into difficult times again under the 'Crisis of the Third Century (AD 235 – 84)' that was characterised by invasion, civil war, plague and economic depression. This crisis was finally brought to an end when Diocletian (Emperor AD 284 – 305) came to power. He made the critical decision to split control of the Empire into a 'tetrachy', or a four way division of power each area under control of an individual emperor. This arrangement was highly successful for some time as it allowed each individual leader to concentrate on the problems of a smaller area, thus regaining and maintaining control. Eventually though, Emperor Constantine 1st 'The Great' took overall leadership of the entire Roman Empire moving the capital to the site of the ancient Greek city of Byzantium, the modern day Istanbul, in AD 330 and naming it Constantinople. This shift of power effectively split the Empire into two distinct divisions, the failing west and the east that grew inexorably to become the Eastern Roman, or the powerful Byzantine Empire. Many historians see the date AD 330 and the establishment of the Byzantine Empire as the beginning point of the Medieval Age, not in the least because of Constantine the Great's conversion to and public support of Christianity.

At what point the new religion took a hold in Malta has been debated, with some making reference to the shipwreck of St Paul on the island in AD 60 as related in the Bible as a possible date;

'*There was a total of 276 of us on board. After everyone had eaten enough they lightened the ship by throwing all the wheat into the sea. When day came, the sailors did not recognize the coast, but they noticed a bay with a beach and decided that, if possible, they would run the ship aground there. So they cut off the anchors and let them sink into the sea.*

The Shipwreck. *When day came, the sailors did not recognize the coast, but they noticed a bay with a beach and decided that, if possible, they would run the ship aground there. So they cut off the anchors and let them sink in the sea and at the same time they untied the ropes that held the steering oars. Then they raised the sail at the front of the ship so that the wind would blow the ship forward, and we headed for shore. But the ship hit a sandbank and went aground; the front part of the ship got stuck and could not move, while the back part was being broken into pieces by the violence of the waves. The soldiers made a plan to kill all the prisoners in order to keep them from swimming ashore and escaping. But the army officer wanted to save Paul, so he stopped them from doing this. Instead, he ordered all the men that could swim to jump overboard first and swim ashore; the rest were to follow holding onto the planks or some broken pieces of the ship. And this is how we all got safely shore.*

In Malta. *When we were safely ashore, we learnt that the island was called Malta. The natives there were very friendly to us. It had started to rain and was cold, so they lit a fire and made us all welcome. Paul gathered together a number of sticks and was putting them on the fire when a snake came out on account of the heat and* *fastened itself to his hand. The natives saw the snake hanging on Paul's hand and said to one another, this man must be a murderer, but fate will not let him live, even though he escaped from the sea. But Paul shook the snake off into the fire and was not harmed at all. They were waiting for him to swell up or suddenly fall down dead. But after waiting for a long time and not seeing anything unusual happen to him, they changed their minds and said 'he is a God'! Not far from that place we saw some fields that belonged to Pablius, the chief official of the island. He welcomed us kindly and for three days we were his guests. Pablius' father was in bed, sick with fever and dysentery. Paul went into his room, prayed, placed his hands on him, and healed him. When this happened all the other sick people on the island came and were healed. They gave us many gifts and when we sailed, they put on board what we needed for the voyage. After three months we sailed away on a ship from Alexandria, called 'the Twin Gods', which had spent the winter in the island.* (Good News Bible, The Acts of The Apostles, 27:37-44 & 28:1-11)

Whether or not Paul began a Christian movement of any sort during his enforced three month stay in Malta is not known and there is no evidence of such a following, but then any such early church would have had to meet in secret to avoid persecution. The earliest date for the arrival of Christianity will never be known but the official one must be when Malta and Gozo, together with Sicily were incorporated into the Byzantine Empire in AD 535 by Emperor Justinian 1st. The years between Constantine's move east to Constantinople in AD 330 and 535 are clouded in darkness but it is probable that the Maltese islands were invaded and occupied twice during the period, first by the Vandals around AD 445 and by the Ostrogoths some 30 years or so later.

Chapter 3

Malta's Medieval History
(AD 535 – 1430)

Maltese history went through an extremely dark period during the two centuries that past between Constantine moving the Roman seat of power to Constantinople in AD 330 and the island being taken back into the then Byzantine Empire by Justinian in AD 535. Everyday life would have changed little as the Roman administration slowly broke down with trade and agriculture continuing much as it had for hundreds of years. Having assumed the responsibility for law and order the disaffection of Roman forces usually leaves a vacuum in an increasingly discarded territory and the indigenous society are often left to fend for themselves. This often shows itself in the reinforcement of properties or the formation of defensive walled settlements but it is not known to what extent this occurred in Malta. Eventually the power gap was filled by Germanic tribes from the east; firstly the Vandals and then the Ostrogoths who would have regarded Malta as a strategic advantage position and would have had little interest in settling on the islands.

Byzantine Empire
(AD 535 – 870)

At the turn of the sixth century, whilst Malta and Gozo were under the control of the Ostrogoths, the Byzantine Emperor 'Justinian the Great' (Emp'r AD 527 – 565) was planning to rebuild the Empire by retaking the lost western provinces. Justinian chose his greatest General, Belisarius, to undertake the task which he carried out to great affect. After crushing the Vandals in North Africa in 533 he retook Sicily, together with Malta and Gozo in 535, before crossing over to the Italian main land and beginning with Naples, headed north capturing lost territories en route until finally recovering Rome.

The appearance of Byzantine forces on Maltese soil would not have produced the usual characteristics of invasion or occupation as Rome had first arrived in Malta in 218 BC at the end of the Second Punic War, as covered above. All the infrastructure of Roman society had been developing over the previous 750 years and the culture had pretty much engrained itself into the everyday life of the islands. So what affect did reoccupation have on life in Malta? Firstly the gap left by any higher echelon Romans from administration, government and the military that might have left the islands to return to the Italian mainland with the arrival of the Germanic forces, would have been refilled. This would have effectively reinstated a level of order whilst the aspect of law and the keeping of the peace, that would have been a part of living under a Roman regime, would have returned.

After this initial resettlement period, the final stand of the Byzantine Empire lasting around 335 years, could be seen as following these stages; firstly normal Roman rule, then steady decline and the end of Byzantine Africa, followed by gradual withdrawal from the islands with an increase of Muslim power in the Mediterranean and then Muslim rule from the year 870.

The towns of Melite on Malta and Gaulos on Gozo remained the largest areas of inhabitation which, whilst initially experiencing times of increased prosperity after 535, as indicated by high amounts of pottery remains from the period, would have suffered from increasing emigration from the onset of the 7th century. The layer of the population that could have packed up and left the islands as times got difficult would have included business leaders, having an adverse effect on trade and many villas would have also been abandoned across rural areas. From Arab accounts of having to dismantle fortifications in Melite it would appear that the city had been well-reinforced against attack and that there would have been a much increased military presence. Excavation at the Xara Palace and on Triq IL Villegaignon, one of the major thoroughfares in Mdina (ancient Melite), revealed such fortifications as a moat and double-skinned curtain wall made from huge bricks of worked rock, all suggesting a well fortified town from the 7th century onwards.

The extent of coastal fortifications is uncertain, but they probably grew up around the bays that would have remained vitally important for trade and military shipping. Ports on the north coast provided access to Sicily and the northern Mediterranean trade routes, whilst the old bay of Marsaxlokk providing sheltered access to the east, was overlooked and protected by the ancient Tas-Silġ holy site. But how much the early religions were still being practiced and for how long is again a matter for discussion as the introduction of Christianity as the official religion of the Byzantine Empire would not have had an immediate effect on a populace with religious traditions going back thousands of years.

There is no documented evidence of Christianity on Malta before the 4th Century but by the 6th Century, during the Byzantine Period, it took hold and began to thrive with the usual well-established church hierarchy. It was Pope Gregory the Great (Pope 590 – 604), who first mentioned an official church on Malta in a series of four letters written between July 592 and January 603 and these, being the only Papal communications about Malta during the Byzantine Period, provide invaluable evidence. From the Pope's correspondence we can understand that the church by this time had become interlocked with central control and ecclesiastical politics and that the Maltese diocese was either under the control of the larger Sicilian church or was subservient to the same Bishop. In fact it was mentioned that a Sicilian Monk by the name of Traianus was to be promoted to Bishop of the island. Whether this appointment was to help resolve problems in the Sicilian and Maltese church is not said but it is clear that there was trouble to be resolved. Pope Gregory spoke of a Bishop Lucillus who was to be removed from power and the church leaders, including Trajanus as Bishop of Malta, were to accept a 'Hadrianus' as Proctor, or 'stand in' for the Pope, to instil church discipline. He states that any Bishop found to be acting in a manner unbecoming of the church would be admonished in secret but that Hadrianus would be reporting back to him of any repeat offenders. On top of all this Malta had connections to the African Church, who owned land on the island and to whom the payment of taxes or rent was to be made.

Ancient rock-cut burial tombs are scattered around the islands, including those at Salina Bay and the Abbattija tad-Dejr, St Paul's and St Agatha's Catacombs in present day Rabat. They are the culmination of centuries of burials joined together to produce huge interconnected complexes of chambers, which developed into extremely impressive early Christian sites. Areas were also carved out to create subterranean churches containing Christian carving and also Jewish art suggesting the presence of such a community in Melite. The wonderful painted walls and fresco in St Agatha's Catacombs are remarkable and well worth a visit.

Row of rock cut catacombs at St Paul's, Rabat

Muslim expansion took on some intensity from the end of the late 7th and early 8th century negatively affecting trade in the area and depressing the economy and this was only confounded by the plague spreading around the Mediterranean. From the early ninth century the amount of attacks by Islamic forces grew massively and with Sicily in sight the strategic position of Malta soon became apparent as had been recognised throughout history by past powers looking to control the Central Mediterranean. Many surrounding islands and territories were taken during this extraordinary growth of Islam in the 9th Century and fighting for the control of Sicily went on for decades until finally Syracuse collapsed after a nine month siege in May 878. Malta, being the last bastion of Byzantium in the area, fought off an attack in 869 but fell the following year to come under Muslim control.

Arab Muslim Period
(870 – 1090)

The so called Arab-Byzantine wars (780-1180) had been raging around the Mediterranean for nearly 100 years when Muslim forces, under the Abbasid Caliphate (750-1258) which was the 3rd Caliphate after the Prophet Muhammad, took Sicily in 827. This was a vitally important strategic foothold that provided protection from the still Byzantine controlled Italian mainland. Originating from the Arabian peninsular, Muslims had occupied Byzantine territories to the west along the coasts of North Africa and Spain and after taking Sicily, Malta was an important target but it took many battles in the area before they ransacked the island in 870. Much of the information that we have from this time is from Muslim texts and one al-Himyarī stated that the islands of Malta remained uninhabited for some time after they had been won. If this is the case the battle must indeed have been ferocious and the Maltese/Byzantium inhabitants were either removed from the island or killed. Whether any Muslim population was already resident on the island is not mentioned in the Arab text, but evidence from the St Paul's catacomb carvings suggests Jewish, as well as Christian usage of the site, so in this spirit of religious tolerance it is at least possible that an early Muslim population may have existed on Malta.

On landing, the Muslim occupiers ransacked the city of Melite, taking down the defences and removing stone columns and other carvings to take back to Sousse, in Tunisia. The invaders must have left an occupation force on Malta, at least, to protect sea trading and to prevent it from becoming a centre of piracy or from being reclaimed by the Byzantine navy. If a population of some sort did remain on Malta records from Muslim or Byzantine sources now go quiet for some time but whether or not Malta was deserted for some years, a large Muslim population eventually grew on the island and remained present until the eleventh century. Not surprisingly, they chose the Roman town of Melite as their capital, renaming it Mdina and rebuilding it into a fine civic centre. Pottery remains from the period indicate the presence of some sort of rural dwelling but it is not certain whether new housing was constructed or if the new occupiers merely moved into deserted Roman villas.

Even with the increase and development of Muslim settlement on Malta the Mediterranean area remained volatile and Byzantine forces never gave up efforts to retake the island. al-Himyarī tells the tale of such an attack;

After the year 440 AH (1048–9 AD), the Muslims populated it and they built its city. Then it became a finer place than it was before. In the year 445 (1053-4), the Byzantines attacked it with many ships and in great numbers, and they besieged the Muslims in the city and the siege became unbearable to them and they were hoping to take them. The Muslims asked them for mercy and the refused it except fir women and belongings. The Muslims reckoned that the number of combatants among themselves and they found them to be about 400. Then they counted their slaves and found that they were more numerous than themselves. They summoned them and said: "If you are loyal to us in our struggle against the enemy and you go as far as we go, and end up where we do, you will be free men; we shall raise you to our level and we shall give you our daughters in marriage, and we shall make you partners in our riches. But if you hesitate and abandon us, your fate will be the same captivity and bondage which will be ours. Indeed, you will fare even worse because with us you may be redeemed by a dear friend or freed by his ally or saved by the support of the community." The slaves, of their own accord, promised more than the Muslims had thought they would, and they (the Muslims) found that the slaves rushed against their enemy more promptly than themselves. When the enemy woke up on the second day, the Byzantines came towards them early as is their custom, hoping on that day to overcome them and take them prisoners. But the Muslims had prepared themselves very well to face them and they came up early to fight them as by premonition. They asked for the help of Allah the Almighty, and they marched and stormed around them piercing them with spears and striking them with swords, without fear or faltering confident of obtaining either of two fine goals: a quick victory or the triumph of the hereafter. Allah the Exalted provided them with help and gave them patience….and the enemy fled defeated without looking back, and the majority of them were massacred. The Muslims took possession of their ships and only one of these slipped away. Their slaves reached the same state of their free men, and they were given what had been promised to them. After that, the enemy feared them and none of the enemy showed up for some time. (Brincat, Joseph, M. *Malta 870–1054. Al-Himyari's account and its linguistic implication.* Pg 11).

This interesting account may appear a little one-sided but it does provide some fascinating insight into Maltese life during the Muslim occupation. It shows that there existed at least two classes of people in the society, freemen and slaves. Where the slaves originated from is not clear; they may have been brought to the island to serve the freemen and to build infrastructure or they may have been Byzantine citizens captured during the invasion. The pragmatic nature of both sides in the face of collective danger gives some indication as to the depth of this class system as the slaves in effect climbed the social ladder by fighting alongside their previous owners. If the slaves were Christians captured during the campaigns and it only took an agreement to free them, then the Muslims must have viewed them as simply prisoners and not as social inferiors.

In the face of ongoing Byzantine military campaigns to recover Malta in the mid 11th century it would have been reasonable to assume that if the island was to return to Christian control it would be as part of the Eastern Roman Empire. Political interplays around the Mediterranean Basin though were complex with many variables and it turned out to be the Normans who finally succeeded in taking over Malta, in 1090, in an invasion that completed a conquest of Sicily that had been underway for over thirty years.

Malta's Norman Conquest
(1091 – 1194)

The Normans could trace their ancestry back to the Viking raiders of Scandinavia and having based themselves in Norman France they named their new homeland after their roots and so Norseman became Norman. From Normandy they expanded their frontiers and those of us that trace our roots back to Britain will know all about the date 1066 and the Battle of Hastings, one of the most important events in the long history of our islands. It was on that day that William I, 'the Bastard Duke of Normandy', beat King Harold II's much depleted army to bring about the 'Norman Conquest' of England.

It was then 25 years later that a branch of the Norman dynasty found themselves in Italy, probably after paying a visit to the Holy Land, but there are conflicting stories as to why these knights made the decision to get involved with Italian politics towards the end of the eleventh century. But for whatever reason they ended up in the south of Italy and from here they eventually set about the 'Conquest of Sicily' (1061-1091), of which Malta was a part. Having been within the Byzantine Empire, Sicily had been invaded by Arab Muslim forces (see above) and the greatly Christian population was now under Muslim control. The Norman knight Robert Guiscard was made 'Duke of Sicily' by the Pope in an obvious effort to encourage him to invade the island and bring it back into Christendom. Plans for invasion were drawn up with Roger Bosso, his younger brother, who was to become Count Roger I and was later known as 'The Great Count'.

Beginning with the short sea crossing from Reggio Calabria, right on the toe of Italy, they occupied Messina and from here the Sicilian campaign was to be relentless. This initial foothold provided the perfect strategic advantage of control over the channel of Messina, the narrowest stretch of sea between Sicily and mainland Italy. From here Robert and Roger's Norman forces moved across the island taking town after town, Palermo fell in 1071, with its fortified citadel following in January 1072, then Trapani fell in 1077, Taormina in 1079, Catania in 1081, Syracuse in 1086 and finally with the occupation of Noto in 1091 Sicily was a Norman territory. This only left the Maltese islands on the Norman wish list. It was later in 1091 that Count Roger set sail for Malta and Gozo to fulfil a task that was in many ways a forgone conclusion, the island's Muslim administration would have watched on as the Norman Counts undertook the slow takeover of Sicily and would have realised that there was no way out. On the other hand the Christian underclass, whether slaves or servants, would have been waiting for the Normans to land and the liberation they would bring. The conquest of Malta, being in many ways a civilised operation, with terms negotiated and agreed, was told splendidly by the Benedictine monk and Norman historian, Geoffrey Malaterra, (translated by Professor Graham Loud);

With trumpets sounding on his order and many other sorts of musical instrument playing, depending on the skills of the player, the anchors were raised and after careful preparation they set sail: on the second day, with the help of a favourable wind, they reached Malta. The count's ship had sailed faster than the others and was the first to reach land. He and thirteen knights disembarked, mounted their horses and attacked the great host of the local inhabitants which had come to the shore to meet them and bar their way. The count killed a number of them, the rest fled, and he pursued them for a considerable distance, cutting down the stragglers. Returning from the pursuit in the evening, he lodged that night on the sea shore with the rest of his army. At daybreak the next morning he marched to the town and laid siege to it, sending out foraging parties all over the island. Neither the Caid who ruled over the town and the island, nor his fellow citizens, were accustomed to military activities, and they were terrified by the presence of their enemies. They requested, of their own free will, a safe conduct so that they might come and discuss matters with the count: he agreed and they came to his tent to ask him for peace terms. [To begin with] they talked around the subject, but finally they realised that they could not deceive this shrewd prince. At the count's request they first of all released the large number of Christian prisoners whom they held within the town, and they offered the count horses and mules, all the weapons they had, and a huge sum of money. They specified what annual payment they would make, promised that the town would be obedient to the count, made oaths according to their own law, and bound themselves to him. The Christian prisoners left the city, shedding tears of joy and moved to the depths of their hearts by their freedom, holding crosses in their right hands made of wood or reeds, whatever each of them found first, singing the Kyrie 75 Eleyson, and [then] flung themselves at the count's feet. Seeing this, our men were bathed in floods of tears by such a pious sight. Having thus bound the city to himself, the count took the prisoners away and embarking them on the ships made a speedy, if very anxious, return, for the weight of the captives was such that he was afraid of sinking. But the right hand of God, so we believe, was revealed in this event, supporting the ships on the waves and bearing them a cubit higher in the ocean, as if they weighed less than on the outward journey. As he hurried home across the sea, he saw away in the distance an island called Gozo, and he turned his sails in that direction with the intention of conquering it. Landing there, he attacked and ravaged it: knowing that by this means he would secure its surrender and place *it under his lordship. From there he sailed safely on to Sicily, bringing back with him a huge haul of booty for his faithful subjects who awaited him. He also brought back the prisoners whom he had rescued from their captivity. Gathering them all together, he set them free, and offered those who wished to remain with him in Sicily a village which he would have built at his own expense at a place of their choosing, and for which he would provide everything necessary for its endowment, also at his own expense: it would be called 'Villafranca', that is a free village, which would be exempted from all tribute or servile exaction in perpetuity. Those who wanted to see their own fields and friends once more he gave permission to go where they pleased, allowing them supplies throughout his lands and free passage across the Straits of Messina. The latter joyfully rendered thanks to God and the count for their freedom, and then they all returned home through a number of different countries, depending on where their native lands were, enhancing the count's reputation far and wide.* (Malaterra, Geoffrey, *The Deeds of Count Roger of Calabria & Sicily & of Duke Robert Guiscard his brother*, (translated by Graham A. Loud) bk 4. Sec 16. pg 74.)

From 1091 Malta was under the control of the Norman Counts based in Palermo but it cannot be certain for how long and how deeply the treaties were followed; after all as long as tributes kept rolling in and the island was operating peacefully, that would probably have been sufficient. It is extremely difficult though to inflict such massive upheaval on a society without causing some problems. Malta changed overnight from being a Muslim state to that of Latin Christianity, under the Papacy, but we are told by Malaterra that Count Roger removed a great many of the Christians immediately after its conquest. This would not have been an ideal strategy for creating a Christian society on Malta as a great proportion of the population would have been Muslims or Jews or followers of the Greek Church. Maybe it was the accommodation of these disparate groups that produced the culture of religious and ethnic tolerance that prevailed on the islands at that time. An attempt was made to bring together the religious groups by incorporating Muslim units into the Norman armies and allowing others to create a free workforce and to ply for paid work. Sea trade on Malta would have continued as it had for hundreds of years and farming activity was plentiful with abundant green pasture land and much production of fruit and honey. Long abandoned carved stone apiaries can still be found today hidden away on Maltese hillsides. An open field system was in operation on the island at the time and rural farmsteads would have existed around the islands for those brave citizens who would be willing to work the land under the constant threat of piracy.

With time more formalised administrative and religious structures would have formed and the whole of Sicily would have been divided into ecclesiastical sees, with specific hierarchies of priests, bishops, and abbots all under the Papal Rule. This, together with more formal legal and general administrational organisation, would have put greater pressure on the Muslim population, who would have felt a reduced status under the new regime of church led feudal leadership. It is probable that many of the more wealthy Muslim families would have left the islands for North Africa at this point.

On Christmas Day, 1130 Count Roger II was crowned King of Sicily, further formalising the Norman control system but with the seat of power being so far away in Palermo, day to day control of Malta may have become a problem outside the main cities of Mdina and Rabat on Gozo. With the increasing threat of Barbary piracy in the Mediterranean area, the tend would have been to live safely within the city walls if possible and many of the diverging nobility built themselves large houses and palaces within the safety of the city walls.

Towards the end of the 12th century the Norman dynasties began to show cracks in their power base allowing the build up of Muslim insurgency forces, based in the Sicilian Mountains who began to directly attack the centre of Norman command in Palermo. Then with the death of King William II, without legitimate heir, internal wars amongst the ruling families broke out leading to the effective end of 103 years of Norman rule of Sicily and therefore Malta.

The Swabian House of Hohenstaufen
(1194 – 1266)

On the death of King William II of Sicily, in 1189, the natural line of succession was not obvious and although it was immediately claimed by William's illegitimate cousin, Tancred of Lecce, this was to be a temporary arrangement. Henry VI, the Holy Roman Emperor, contended the throne of Sicily citing his marriage to Constance, the daughter of Roger II of Sicily and he took the throne in 1194. This agreement meant that there was a bloodline connection with William through Constance, whilst the line of Sicilian Kings would pass to the House of Hohenstaufen, a powerful dynasty of German monarchs, based in Swabia.

The reign of Henry VI lasted only three years and on his death in 1197 the crown was passed onto Frederick II (26th December 1194 – 13th December 1250), Henry's three year old son. The next ten years were characterized by internecine warfare, during which time Frederick was passed through the care of one Regent and at least two guardians but he grew up to have a truly increasable life. During his period of sovereignty he became strong enough to act against the Papacy with a list of titles including; King of Sicily (1197-1250), Duke of Swabia (1228-1235), King of Germany (1212-1250), Holy Roman Emperor (1220-1250) and King of Jerusalem (1229-1243).

Whilst the career of Frederick II is a fascinating subject in its own right, it falls outside the range of our subject matter, especially when considering that in contrast to the extremely wide ranging nature of his activities the islands of Malta and Gozo would have been reduced to little more than an insignificance.

We saw in the previous section that political control from the central power in Palermo had been losing its effectiveness towards the end of the Norman Period and with the enthronement of the child king Frederick this situation was only exacerbated. On Malta the perceived power vacuum would have attracted increased pirate activity and throughout the kingdom the Muslim population, which had felt repressed under Norman control, became organised. The Muslim leader Ibn Abbied moved his people into out of town settlements and began to construct fortresses to protect and expand 'Sicilian Islam', a state within a state. In November 1198 the Chancery of the royal palace issued a charter addressed to all of the citizens of Malta and Gozo whether Christian or Muslim to reaffirm that the islands were under direct royal government, 'as it was under the reign of Good King William'. This was, of course, an attempt to regain peaceful control by the king in Palermo. To the same aim Tancred of Lecce had introduced the new office of 'Count of Malta', beginning with Margarito da Brindisi in 1192, followed by Guglielmo Grasso, a Genoese pirate, in 1197.

The Maltese Counts did not seem to spend a great deal of time actually on the islands but they did appear to go some way to achieving King Frederick's goal of peace by central control, although the position did seem to be its own power base for the various activities of the counts. The next in line was 'Enrico Pescatore', or Henry the Fisherman (1203-1232) another Genoese pirate who used Malta for just that activity as well as a base for his wish to create a 'kingdom of Crete'. In 1212 Frederick paid Henry a visit at his base in Genoa, where he awarded the count the right to mint Maltese coinage.

As Frederick built his power base the issue of Muslim rebellion eventually had to be faced, the king was known to respect the laws and way of life of Muslims but uprising and insurgency was another matter. Malta had been declared as within the 'Royal Demise', or under legal ownership of the King of Sicily and this included the people living there. In 1229 Frederick began the process of active removal of Muslims from the land and resituating them in prescribed towns. In Malta, of the estimated 250,000 Muslims, at least 40,000 were removed, many to Lucera in Southern Italy, some maybe sold as slaves on the North African coast. Any lack of manpower problem caused by this process of active removal was solved by the introduction of new Christians from colonies and from penal resettlement. Eventually the conversion of Muslims to Christianity took on a tremendous pace but although much of this was state manufactured it probably made little difference to day to day life on the islands. A much reduced Muslim community remained in Malta and continued to be an important part of the culture and the development of the language, which can still be seen in the place and street names on the island.

Administrational control became the norm in Malta, in what had become a sophisticated state under Frederick II and accounts of the islands population, overall income and expenditure were being officially recorded at least by 1240, as such a document, completed by Giliberto Abbate, the local administrator for the crown, has been uncovered.

It was also Frederick II who encouraged falconry in Malta, because of his great interest in the activity and he organised many falcon hunting expeditions on the islands. These were elaborate affairs, including a massive entourage, that would last for months at a time. Frederick also wrote what is regarded as a leading treatise on the subject of falconry, a lengthy work which he dedicated to his son Manfred. This was just one more achievement to add to the mass of accomplishments of Frederick II in his reign that lasted more than half a century until his death in 1250 and that left Malta and Gozo much more stable and established mini-states.

Frederick II was succeeded by his son Conrad but he died in 1254, only four years into office and the crown was past to his two year old son Conrad II, who lost it on appeal to Frederick's son Manfred in 1258. At this time 'Nicoloso' had been Count of Malta for nearly 30 years and he was feeling increasingly disenfranchised in respect to Palermo and set about organising a revolt to claim control of Malta in the name of Genoa. Manfred though proved up to the task of reclaiming the island through negotiations, which gave Nicoloso all his previous status and rights of office and improved trading terms. This turned out to be a temporary arrangement that lasted no more than three years as unbeknown to the Sicilian authorities, Pope Urban IV had awarded the kingship of Sicily to Charles of Anjou, whilst of course Manfred was still on the throne. It was on 26th February 1266 at the battle of Benevento that the two sides met and that Manfred lost his life and the House of Hohenstaufen lost the throne of Sicily.

The Capetian House of Anjou
(1266 – 1283)

Arms of the Capetian House of Anjou

Having beaten King Manfred at the battle of Benevento in 1266 and then his brother Conradin at the battle of Taglicozzo in 1268, Charles of Anjou (21 March 1227–7 January 1285) ruled over the kingdom of Sicily and therefore Malta, for this 17 year period. Charles was from the House of Capet, the ruling dynasty of France, his father was King Louis VIII 'The Lion' (r1223-1226), his mother Blanche of Castile and his elder brother King Louis IX of France (r1226-1270). The line of Counts of Anjou were given the name of Angevin after the

Anjou area of north-western France that contained the town of Angers and that today is part of the Pays de la Loire.

Also holding the titles of Count of Provence, Roman Senator and Signore of Tuscany, Charles was known for his strict leadership and his preference for tight control over events and on gaining the kingship of Sicily he moved its capital to Naples. This in itself would seem an intelligent strategy that would provide a clean start with trusted personnel untainted by the previous Hohenstaufen regime, but it did not go down well in Sicily and caused serious resentment right at the beginning of his reign. On taking control of Sicily, Charles kept the majority of the existing administrative procedures in place, undoubtedly to avoid confusion, but he greatly tightened enforcement policies. This heavy-handed attitude again caused popular resentment, leading to unrest that was, again, immediately quashed.

An examination of Malta and Gozo during the period of Charles of Anjou is much clearer than in previous periods due to the greater availability of official records kept mainly by local government. Tax policy and law were recorded in great depth and it is clear that the tax burden laid on the people on Malta, which grew significantly during this period, was another cause of great conflict. In 1276 the Maltese people refusing to pay certain taxes and ignoring all reminders from royal envoys, created a situation where the Naples government had to issue instructions to their local representatives to intervene swiftly.

Central government upheld the offices of Procurator and Chief Castellany (castrum maris) that mainly had the responsibility for the island's castles but in effect appeared to hold much local power on behalf of Naples. Bertrand de Real, who held this office from August 1270 to July 1274, was accused by the people of Malta of aggressively disregarding the islander's land rights, the outcome of which being a demand by central government that redress had to be paid to the people. This fairer element of Charles's government again indicated a strict adherence to the detail of the law and other successful examples of private petitions to central government are recorded. In 1071 the people of Malta petitioned in respect of vacant land on the islands that would have been owned by the royal purse and won the right to rent this land, thus bringing it back into general usage.

The population of the islands would appear to have reached a level of religious cohesion with any remaining Muslims pretty much integrated into Christianity, an organisation with a well defined hierarchy and which was exempt from the payment of taxes. A problem had developed though in the area of Genoese interests as personified by Nicoloso, Count of Malta, who may have felt his office to have lost relevance with the elevation of other royal positions and an invasion of the islands took place in 1274 that devastated the population of Gozo.

It was Charles's strict, heavy-handed approach to leadership and taxation that resulted in his eventual loss of the Kingdom of Sicily as a result of what became known as the 'War of the Sicilian Vespers'. This is the first time in the history of the Sicilian Kingdom that a popular uprising has brought down its ruling power. On the surface it may appear that this revolt resulted from a single incident, but of course this is never the case in such situations and what is witnessed as a spontaneous outburst is, in fact, the blowing of a gasket releasing years of built up pressure. The people put up with Charles's oppressive regime only for so long before they had had enough. They saw themselves in increasing poverty through increasing taxes that disappeared to the absent French king to pay for his private wars that showed no benefits to the Sicilian islands.

The initial incendiary incident took place at the Church of the Holy Spirit on the outskirts of Palermo during the 'Vespers', or sunset prayers, on Easter Monday, 30th March 1282. As the story goes, many were gathered at the church when a few French soldiers, obviously worse the wear from drink, joined them and began showing unwanted advances towards a married woman. Her husband then took his knife and killed Drouet, the French officer and when his comrades tried to intervene they were also killed. This event sparked off a night of vicious rioting, as described by Steven Runciman;

'To the sound of the bells messengers ran through the city calling on the men of Palermo to rise against the oppressor. At once the streets were filled with angry armed men, crying "Death to the French" ("Moranu li Franchiski" in their Sicilian dialect). Every Frenchman they met was struck down. They poured into the inns frequented by the French and the houses where they dwelt, sparing neither man, woman nor child. Sicilian girls who had married Frenchmen perished with their husbands. The rioters broke into the Dominican and Franciscan convents; and all the foreign friars were dragged out and told to pronounce the word "ciciri", whose sound the French tongue could never accurately reproduce. Anyone who failed the test was slain... By the next morning some two thousand French men and women lay dead; and the rebels were in complete control of the city.' (Runciman, Steven, *Sicilian Vespers: A History of the Mediterranean World in the Later Thirteenth Century*, pg 212.)

The insurgency spread from Palermo right around Sicily until after six weeks all but Messina had been recovered by the rebels. By the 28th April even the superior defences of this town had been overcome and the royal fleet had been burned in the harbour. The islanders, wishing to be recognised as a free state under the protection of the church, sent ambassadors to Pope Martin IV requesting this, but unfortunately for them, the Pope still championed Charles and instructed the Sicilians to hand power back to him. On hearing this they petitioned King Pedro III of Aragon who was connected back to the previously opposed line of the House of Hohenstaufen through his wife Constance, Manfred's daughter and heir to 'Good King' Fredrick II. Being amicable to the Sicilian request, Pedro sent a fleet of war ships to Trapani and landing on 30th August 1282, made his way east by road to Palermo with his fleet following by sea, arriving on 2nd September. After promises to the Sicilian people of fair treatment, his leadership was accepted and he was crowned king Peter I of Sicily two days later. This was just one more title for the powerful Pedro of Aragon and although Charles attempted the reinvasion of Sicily on a number of occasions, he was no competition for King Peter and never made a successful landing.

Whilst this concluded the takeover with both Sicily and Malta swearing allegiance to King Peter in 1282, there still remained the problem of the Angevin occupation of the Castrum Maris (sea castle) at the head of the Maltese Grand Harbour, led by Matthew de Podio. In February 1283 the new regime attempted to appease the Angevins by appointing the Catalan, Huget de Cambrils to provide a safe withdrawal of the militia. In the same year King Peter renewed an 1198 charter confirming that Malta and Gozo were incorporated into the royal demesne and under its dominion, whilst reaffirming all of the privileges given to the islands but still the Angevin presence remained in the Castrum. Then in April 1283 a prominent supporter of King Peter, Manfred Lancia, was appointed to the position of Captain and Justiciar of the Maltese islands.

The Angevin navy, being ensconced in the Castrum Maris, still had control of the Maltese Grand Harbour, a situation that could not be allowed to continue now that the islands were supposed to be under Argonese rule. The effort to resolve this predicament, that took place on 8th July 1283, became known as the 'Battle of Malta'. The Angevin Admiral, William Cornuit entered the harbour with a fleet of around 25 French galleons, to reinforce the Castrum Maris. Manfred Lancia in pursuit with a fleet, learned that their opponents had tried to take the castle in Gozo and failed and were now taking cover in the Grand Harbour. Lancia prepared for battle and waited until dusk before entering the harbour and engaging William's fleet and the Castrum that was garrisoned by one hundred men. The battle of Malta raged for a whole day until Lancia emerged as the clear victor. Manfred then moved his men-at-arms to Mdina and placed it under siege. The town was apparently already loyal to the new royal administration but it was held until they again confirmed their loyalty to King Peter in what appears to have been a belt –and-braces strategy.

If a firm date was to be fixed for the Catalan/Argonese takeover of Malta and Gozo, then the 8th July 1283, with their victory at the Battle of Malta would seem to be the ideal choice. But as is usual for the history of Medieval warfare, this was not the end of the matter.

The House of Aragon
(1283 – 1530)

King Pedro II of Aragon

After the 1283 Battle of Malta control of the islands was placed firmly in the regal hands of King Pedro II of Aragon (King Peter of Sicily) but this was only the beginning of a confusing theatre of military and diplomatic events. In the first half of 1287 a fleet of French Angevin ships re-entered the Maltese Grand Harbour, recapturing the sea castle (Castrum Maris) and some occupied land. In retaliation the Aragonese Manfred Lancia captured up to 50 Flemish galleys, killing around 5,000 people during the battle. Meanwhile the Angevin leader King Charles II was being held prisoner by the Aragonese and it was James II of Aragon (King Peter's son and successor), that organised a diplomatic agreement to give Charles his freedom in exchange for the overall Angevin acceptance of Aragonese rule of the Kingdom of Sicily. As a result Charles formally surrendered the islands to James in October 1288.

At this point the Pope, still favouring Angevin rule of Sicily, intervened to disrupt this apparently successful agreement, giving ownership of the islands of Corsica and Sardinia to James of Aragon in exchange for releasing control of Sicily to Charles II. As described above, the population of Sicily had strenuously rejected Angevin rule with the War of the Vespers and they were not going to accept their return, so they then discarded James in favour of his younger brother Frederick, placing him on the throne in 1296. But it was the next piece in this puzzle that was the most unusual, on hearing the Sicilian decision to replace him with his brother, James declared war on Sicily in order to enforce the agreement with the church to install Angevin rule, the very people the Aragonese had been fighting to remove since his father Peter took over Sicilian rule in 1282. On 13th February 1296 the new King Fredrick made a statement to the effect that the islands had been attacked by James's forces and in Malta whole villages had been burned with many people captured. Never the less Frederick reigned over the kingdom of Sicily for 40 years bringing at least some form of central rule.

His successors though did not maintain this level of royal control and steadily lost influence and reverence as the decades rolled by.

Malta gained some level of distance from the ruling centre when in 1300 Fredrick offered the castle of Malta to the

Genoese counts, who would manage the islands whilst maintaining the Aragonese kings as feudal overlords. This system of kingship was by no means unusual in Medieval Europe and it gave over complete day to day power to local aristocratic families and therefore if any abuse of leadership would arise it would be from that level.

It was Giacomo de Pellegrino, a privateer (or government paid pirate), from Messina in Sicily that dominated Malta's political scene from the early 14th century until 1372. Pellegrino was related to the Counts of Malta by marriage but his rise to power on the island probably came from his intimidatory methods and by 1356 he had taken the post of Captain of the Maltese Islands and by 1357 was Justiciar and Castellan, a position he was awarded for life. In 1360 Frederick made the unusual decision to install Guido Ventimiglia, an outsider, to the post of Count of Malta, possibly under the influence of Pellegrino but he died after two years and they reverted to Manfredo III Chiaramonte Admiral of Sicily, to fill the post. It was clear that Pellegrino had been allowed to wield immense power seemingly untapped, he claimed huge plots of land on Malta, including walled gardens, estates and vineyards and this tax exempt pirate became a money lender, even to royalty. By 1372 Frederick must have decided that Pellegrino had grown too powerful and needed to be removed to restore royal authority to the Maltese islands. Thomas Morchio was deployed from Genoa with 10 galleys to Malta where he lay siege to Pellegrino and his men in the Castrum Maris and Mdina for two months. Morchio found willing help amongst the islanders suggesting that the local population would also be glad to see the back of Pellegrino's power base. In the November all of his assets were confiscated and he was gaoled, only to be released with a pardon after eleven months, when he was exported back to and confined in Messina.

Towards the end of the 14th century the Maltese islands maintained the usual sophisticated administrative offices and procedures and they issued their own monetary currency, distinguishable from that of Sicily. It appears that the islands had separated into a collection of Arab speaking fiefdoms operating independently under the control of a local leader, whist still under the overall kingship of Aragon. The final 20 or 30 years of the 14th century saw hard times as the black plague, having been ravishing Europe and taking around a third of its population, hit Malta followed by terrible harvests with the resulting lack of food and cotton manufacture, a major industry on the island. The poverty and social unrest being the consequence of these factors meant that Papal taxes went unpaid and when the church bailiffs arrived, they described Malta as a miserable place of hunger and mortality and left without being able to collect even the minimum of tithes.

The crowning of Alfonso V 'the Magnanimous' (r. 1416-1456), was not a forgone conclusion and his fight to the Aragonese throne set the stage for many years of battling, much of it with the old enemy the House of Anjou, that culminated in a massive war for the possession of Naples, which he won on the 26th February 1443. Alfonso's constant state of warfare produced a continuing and increasing drain on crown resources, so much that he began to pawn out land and property to finance his campaigns.

Alfonso V 'the Magnanimous'

On the 20th January 1421 an agreement was signed with Antonio de Cardona, the Sicilian Viceroy for the pawning of Malta and Gozo for the payment of 30,000 Aragonese florins. On completion of the deal it turned out that Cardona was actually a legal stand in for one Gonsalvo de Monroy, a Castilian knight and galley captain, who acquired the Lordship with full civil and criminal rights over the islands. As if the lessons learned from the menacing rule of Pellegrino hadn't been sufficient warning, the Maltese islands found themselves again under the control of a single autocrat only accountable to a far off monarch. In the end it was the population of Gozo that, in 1425, first rose up against Monroy, who had by this time become Admiral of Sicily and by the following year this popular insurrection had spread to Malta. Monroy, together with his wife and his militia were blockaded in the Castrum Maris until 1427 when he was released with a promise of the repayment of his 30,000 florins and certain extra payments. On the 20th June 1428 Alfonso also issued a royal charter that became known as 'The Maltese Magna Carta Liberatis', which confirmed that the islands were part of the royal domain and that they had a right to be ruled directly by the crown. After Monroy's death on 12th April 1429, he left 10,000 florins to Alfonso, another 10,000 distributed amongst the population of the islands and had the remaining third written off as he had never received it back. Throughout this whole affair Alfonso had received the initial 30,000 florins for the pawning of the Maltese islands then a further 10,000 on the death of Monroy; the people of the islands received a period of rule by a foreign interloper and 10,000 florins that had originally come from them.

The reality of this renewed vow of royal rule and protection was brought into strict perspective with the surprise attack on the Maltese islands by the Muslim Hafsid of Tunisia in September 1429, who landed with up 70 vessels and 18,000 troops to attack a population of around 10,000, up to one third of which were taken into slavery. This tragic event highlighted the remote position of the Maltese islands in respect to the royal centre of control and also the vulnerability and inadequacy of defences that really only consisted of a local militia and the limited forces based in the Castrum Maris. Whilst a system of watch towers would act as an effective early warning system there was not a great deal that could be done in the case of invasion or localised pirate raiding and this remained the case right up until the occupation of the Knights of St John.

The Muslim attack of 1429 could have resulted in demoralisation and collapse of organised administration on

Malta but on the contrary and quite extraordinarily it became the catalyst for an extremely advanced and effective democratic local government system that would be in place for the next 100 years. Each year the islanders would elect four jurats, or town councillors, who would begin their term of office on the 1st September and at the termination of their period of duty they would provide all records of their activities to both the council and a royal commission for inspection. For a small country that had suffered so much under the hegemony of tyrants the accountability of this form of administration would have provided much needed stability. The jurats would have oversight of a notary and various government employees with the responsibility for running all aspects of the islands administration and filling public positions such as school teachers, pharmacists and barber surgeons.

There were also royal appointments on the islands such as the Captain of Malta, who would be in charge of the criminal justice system and the citizen militia. The 'Castallany' would be responsible for keeping the Castrum Maris garrisoned and ready to go into action and the small 'borgo', or settlement alongside the Grand Harbour both of which were of independent jurisdiction. There was also the Secrezio and Vice-Secrezio, the royal accountants who would balance the financial books after the taking of rents, although income from this area would be decreasing as more land became privately owned. Royal and local authority would come together at regular council meetings run by the Captain, where all could attend and discuss impending issues except for church officials who, as the other independent power on the islands, could only attend if religious matters where on the agenda.

The Maltese people had initiated a form of government that would provide stability on the islands for a whole century and this led to an effective economy and high rates of employment with a fixed rate of pay for workers on other people's land. Produce included cotton, fruit, wine, olive oil, pulses, grain and cotton with fishing as important as it would be for any small island and craft houses, shops and taverns would prepare and sell a whole manner of finished goods. These would be traded in land amongst the islands population or overseas through the practice of sea trade that was so much part of Malta's heritage.

Chapter 4

Knights of St John
(1530 – 1798)

Cross of the Knights of St John

From a Brotherhood to an Order

Whilst the Knights of St John of Jerusalem can be said to have been firmly a product of the Crusades to the Holy Lands, their form as a monastic chivalric order or an order of warrior monks, was more a process of circumstance than by design. They began their days running hospitals in Jerusalem after the crusaders took the city following the successful siege of 1099, under the first leader, Gerard Thom, 'The Blessed Gerard' (gm 1099-1120). Over the proceeding decades a number of Papal bulls, the need to protect people and property together with the increasing threat from encroaching Muslim forces, fashioned the organisation.

Gerard Thom 'The Blessed Gerard' (1099-1120)

In 1135 Pope Innocent II provided the hospital and the 'Brotherhood of St John' with jurisdictional exemption from the crown of Jerusalem, indicating that a brotherhood existed at that time that was recognised by the church and four years later priests were to be allowed to work as part of the hospital. Another important development came with the document 'Christianae fidel religio', issued in October 1154 by Pope Anastasius IV that confirmed the Hospitallers as holding the status of 'Exempt Order of the Church', bringing them directly under papal charge as a recognised 'Order'.

As with the Knights Templar, the Hospitallers began to receive gifts of land and property in return for perceived religious favours and by the middle of the 12th century they had become extremely wealthy. The gift to the Hospitallers of the castle of Bayt Jibrin by King Fulk of Jerusalem in 1135 proved to be significant in the beginnings of a militaristic role for the order. As more such strategic properties were bestowed, some with feudal rights intact, defensive obligations increased exponentially, a duty that was originally met through the employment of mercenary knights. At a general chapter meeting of the Hospitallers held in 1205 by the then leader Alfonso of Portugal, the 'Chivalric Order of St John' was referred to, suggesting that by this time the organisation had developed into a form generally recognised.

Bound together as an order under the three monastic vows of chastity, obedience and poverty, the brothers would be members of the convent (the central structure of the organization) under one of three main divisions. Firstly the Chaplains of Obedience who having taken holy orders would be responsible for running the hospitals and chapels, this would have been the earliest section but their importance reduced until very much eclipsed by their armed brothers the Military Knights who could claim at least four generations of nobility from both parents and who would become the dominant element of the order and finally the third section, the serving brothers who would have been pastoral brothers but would not have been exempt from active military service. Because of the increasing size of the order with members from across Europe, further divisions were created in relation to the language spoken and therefore the eight national groups of Aragon, Provence, Auvergne, Castile, France, Italy, Germany and England (with Scotland and Ireland), were formed. These language based sub-divisions would have their own leadership and be based in their own priories and commanderies, whilst under one overall Grand Master responsible for the running of an independent state with its own currency and diplomatic relations with outside countries.

Refuge in Rhodes

Palace of the Grand Master of the Knights of Rhodes (1844)

The Knights of St John took an active role in the Holy Lands during the time of the Christian occupation with both the military protection of pilgrims and in the running of hospitals. The need for these fundamental functions of the brotherhood appeared to come to an end though in 1291 after the siege of Acre by Muslim forces resulted in the loss of the Holy Lands. With the Knight's position now becoming untenable they reached an agreement with King Henry II of Cyprus to allow them temporary residence in the Cypriot city of Limassol. In keeping with their medical tradition they built a new hospital there and continued with armed protection of Mediterranean shipping routes through increased naval power introduced by Grand Master Foulques de Villaret (GM 1305-1319). This new maritime role was to prove of fundamental importance to the order's future. Then on the 15th August 1309, after much planning and preparation, the Knights of St John captured the island of Rhodes, together with nearby smaller islands and harbours and set up their new Convent in the city of Rhodes itself. This was an intelligent choice for a permanent new home as it provided a renewed role of importance protecting the Eastern Mediterranean and strategic sea routes in all directions. Rhodes soon became a popular and safe stop-off point for pilgrim and cargo ships travelling between Western Europe and Constantinople, Jaffa, Alexandria and Palestine.

Increased new naval pressures meant that the Knights had to abandon many European hospitals apart from a huge new one constructed in Rhodes and focus on maritime protection and the upkeep of the massive amount of estates that had been gifted throughout Europe. The upkeep of so much real-estate and ships together with the cost of meeting military logistics proved to be a huge financial burden on the Convents and whilst the organisation became land rich they became increasingly cash poor. The strategy introduced to even out this discrepancy involved increasing rents and corsairing activities, in other words piracy, against foreign ships in the Mediterranean.

It was against this backdrop that calls for the amalgamation between the two orders of the Templars and the Hospitallers were being heard and Pope Clement V summoned the leaders of both orders to a meeting in Paris, where they were to discuss how this was to be carried out. The Grand Master of the Knights Hospitallers, William de Villaret made the excuse that he was not able to leave the assault on Rhodes, but Jacques de Molay had no such diversion and he was forced to attend the meeting which he probably knew could well be a trap. Behind the scenes King Philippe le Bel of France, who had become massively in debt to the order, had put proceedings in motion and now that he had de Molay on his territory, he sprang an ambush. At dawn on Friday 13th October 1307, the agents of the king opened sealed orders that they had been holding for a month. All the Templars in France, including Jacques de Molay, were arrested under charges of heresy, sodomy, blasphemy and denying Christ. Two papal bulls were consequently issued, 'Vox in Excelso' (22nd March 1312), which dissolved the Templar Order and 'Ad Providam' (2nd May 1312), which confounded Philippe by transferring all the Templar's property to the Hospitallers. Such a massive transfer of wealth would have made the Hospitallers amongst the richest and most powerful organisations in the world with the associated financial pressures. From an order of monks running a hospital the Knights of St John were now a multinational conglomerate.

For the next two hundred years the Knights of St John were based in Rhodes and it was from here that they ran their operations whilst the Ottoman Empire, with its origins in Turkey, had been growing its power base in the Eastern Mediterranean. The Hospitallers had proved a serious irritation to the Ottomans as they had been attacking their ships and confiscating valuable merchandise and commodities so the Turks became determined to permanently remove the Knights from their strategically positioned island. After a defeated invasion in 1480 the Ottoman Çoban Mustafa Pasha approached Rhodes with 400 ships on 26th June 1522 followed by Sultan Suleiman with an army of 100,000 troops on 28th July and they were ready for a long siege. Grand Master Philippe Villiers de L'Isle-Adam (GM 1521-1534) continued an extensive program of renovation and refortification that had begun after the earlier attack of 1480 and an earthquake the following year and the town was highly fortified. The city was surrounded by two, or in some places three, stone walls and the Knights' fleet was waiting in the harbour behind a heavy iron chain that blocked the sea gate and so the scene was set for the stand-off.

The city of Rhodes withheld against siege bombardment for six months until 22nd December when a large portion of the city accepted Suleiman's offer of 12 clear days to vacate the island and on the 1st January 1523 the Knights of St John paraded in full battle armour out of the city, down to the harbour and left the island, again without a home.

Destination Malta

Charles V, Holy Roman Emperor, having a religious association with the Catholic knights allowed them temporary access to Syracuse under his role as King Charles I of Spain and II of Sicily, so this was their first port of call. de L'Isle-Adam remained here for some time whilst the order necessarily began to spread out in order to find accommodation. Over this uncertain time the knights also harboured in Crete, Messina, Civitavecchia, Nice and for a longer time in the Italian town of Viterbo. The Grand Master was becoming worried that the Order would start to naturally disintegrate under the pressure of separation and lack of local leadership and was seeking a new permanent base as a priority. In opposition to all advice de L'Isle-Adam wanted to retake Rhodes and he set off on an expedition around the European courts to raise support for such an attack, where he found none except a gift of guns and cash from King Henry VIII of England.

The offer of a permanent home in Nice was quickly rejected as this would have placed the Knights of St John within a convoluted French political system taking it away from the Orders fundamental goals. Focus then shifted to the islands of Malta and Gozo, which whilst sitting in a strategic position at the centre of the Mediterranean at its narrowest point, would have been under intermittent attack from Barbary pirates. A friendly force in charge of Malta would have solved this difficult situation for Charles and so he offered the islands to the Knights of St John, but with the condition that they also took over control of the city of Tripoli, another of Charles headaches as it was surrounded by the Barbary states of North Africa and thus was proving terribly difficult to defend. If the knights accepted the king's proposal the Mediterranean would have been effectively divided into two with a strong loyal defensive line stretching from Malta to Tripoli to the south.

The Grand Master was not sure whether settling in Malta, Gozo and Tripoli would be a viable prospect so on 13th July 1524 he sent a fact-finding mission to the islands containing representatives from the eight language groups. The commission reported that the islands were of soft sandstone rock, Malta being seven leagues long and three to four wide, with soil to a depth of up to four feet deep, whilst much of the ground was stony and unfit for cultivation. The islanders grew cotton, cumin and fruits, could provide up to four months of food and engaged in goods exchange with Sicily and in sea trade. Water was extremely rare with few running streams that provided for a population of around 12,000 on Malta and 5,000 on Gozo. Malta had the one major city of Mdina and two castles that would be used as places of asylum during pirate raids. On the positive side were the two large and easily defended harbours that would have been ideal to house a naval fleet.

It was on 19th May 1527, at a Chapter General meeting, that the knights decided to accept Charles's offer of the Maltese islands and Tripoli and on 24th May 1530, in Castlefrance, Northern Italy, they were invested in the properties in perpetuity, noble, full and free enfeoffment, on the payment of one falcon to Charles each year. It is important to note that the knights had not conquered the islands and that they held them as a feoffment, or under feudal tenure and that Charles retained sovereignty. In this way he upheld the 'Magna Carta' sworn by King Alfonso V of Aragon, in 1428, stating that the sovereignty of the Islands of Malta would never be transferred away. For better or worse the Knights of St John, led by their Grand Master Philippe Villiers de L'Isle-Adam, sailed into Malta's Grand Harbour on the 26th October 1530 and claimed their new home.

Malta a new island home

Grand Master Philippe Villiers de L'Isle-Adam
(GM 1521-1534)

The official hand over ceremony took place with great pomp on 13th November in the old capital of Mdina, where L'Isle-Adam with his entourage, processed towards the city gate beneath a fine canopy of state and made vows upon the great cross of the cathedral and the cross of the Order of St John. The Grand Master then received the silver keys of the city from Capitano della Verga and the gates were opened to allow him to enter as the island's new leader. Mdina, being the only large centre of population on Malta, had always been the capital city so it would have been expected that the knights would have moved in to run their administration from the existing municipal buildings but this was not to be the case. With naval capability becoming such a fundamental part of the knight's activities, L'Isle-Adam chose the Castrum Maris on the Grand Harbour to build their base and it became clear that the knights were to be an order apart from the island's general populace.

This must have been a time of extreme uncertainty for the Maltese islanders who had been used to a successful method of government put in place in response to the 1429 raid by the Muslim Hafsid (see above – The House of Aragon). Would they be allowed to continue the system of democratic self rule or had they just installed new rulers? Times would not have been easy on the islands, especially for the poor, with farming the land an arduous task and with the constant threat of pirate attack and possible enslavement. The arrival of the knights must have produced mixed feelings, the rich and ruling class may have feared loss of status and power, whilst the less well off may have seen opportunities for new forms of employment and protection from invaders.

The Castrum Maris had served as protection for the Grand Harbour since the Early Medieval Period and now it was to take on a whole new existence as the home for the Knights of St John and so become in effect the new capital city or at least governmental centre, of Malta. The Castrum, together with the village or 'borgo' (le Bourg du Chateau, or village of the castle), that sat next to it to house the castle and naval workers, had enjoyed independent jurisdiction from Mdina and they were to be much renovated, strengthened and fortified against Ottoman and Barbary attack. The knights renamed the Castrum 'Fort St Angelo' and the name borgo developed over time to Birgu as it is today, with its alternative name 'Vittoriosa' that it received after 1565. The knights knew Birgu as 'Citta Nuova', or the new city to distinguish it from Mdina, or 'Citta Vecchia' the old city and they moored their ships in the harbour under its protection, including the pride of the fleet, the Santa Anne.

The Carrack Santa Anne, A 1522 depiction

Launched the day before the knights vacated Rhodes, the Santa Anne was a huge carrack ship, 132 ft long and 40 ft wide, armoured with 50 cannon and many smaller naval guns and with a capability of carrying 500 well equipped soldiers or 4000 tons of cargo as well as her crew. She was fitted out with fine cabins and an officers mess below deck, a forge and blacksmiths shop, a mill and ovens so that bread could be produced whilst at sea and a working garden. The most impressive feature was the vessel's groundbreaking lead-lined hull, designed to stop cannon. It was aboard the Santa Anne that Grand Master de L'Isle-Adam had sailed into the Grand Harbour for the first time.

Having led the knights to a new permanent residence, Philippe Villiers de L'Isle-Adam passed away in 1534 and his two successors Piero de Ponte (GM 1534–1535) and Didier de Saint-Jaille (GM 1535–1536) only managed one year each, so it was left to Grand Master Juan de Homedes (GM 1536–1553) to continue the fortification of Malta. A major attack of combined Ottoman and North African forces hit the major island in 1551 but having little effect moved on to Gozo, where they took around 5,000 slaves before continuing to Tripoli which again was poorly defended and although it took a matter of weeks, Governor Gaspard de Vallier eventually surrendered the city to Sultan Suleiman. Although the position of Tripoli, isolated as it was amongst Barbary controlled North Africa, making it a prime location for attack and with the town's fortifications badly in need of modification and strengthening, the blame for the loss of the city fell on de Vallier and so de Homedes had him imprisoned. It is possible that the Grand Master might have been hauled over the coals by the court of King Charles for not keeping up the original agreement to protect Tripoli as well as Malta, but the loss of this unwanted North African city would not have been long mourned by the knights, who would have seen it as an unnecessary burden.

Grand Master Claude de la Sengle (GM 1553-1557)

Work on Birgu continued and the town grew in size and importance through an increased population and the sea trade, including slaves, that the knights brought and it soon amalgamated with the nearby Bormla (later also known as Citta Cospicus), a village to the inner end of the Birgu peninsula. Expansion under Grand Master Claude de la Sengle (GM 1553-1557), continued with the spread of the city to the old village of Isla, on the opposite peninsula to Birgu, that was renamed Sengea, after him (also known as Citta Invicta). This extended walled city included Fort St Michael built onto the point of the peninsular opposite Fort St Angelo, in order to provide fire power support from the other side of the channel and to help protect the fleet in Dockyard Creek. Today this large urban area with its atmospheric narrow streets that was the original settlement for the knights is known under the combined name of 'The Three Cities'. Also, after the attack of 1551, a further fort was constructed at the head of Mount Sciberras, a peninsular much larger than Birgu and Isla, that lay across the whole of the north side of the Grand Harbour and the south of Marsamxett Harbour. With the added stronghold of Fort St Elmo in place, the knights must have felt more ready to meet invasion but it was the behaviour of the knights themselves that was the main preoccupation of the incoming Grand Master Jean Parisot de Valette (GM 1557-1568).

Grand Master Jean Parisot de Valette (GM 1557-1568)

De Valette had joined the Knights of St John in 1514, at the age of 20 and he was a purist, believing in keeping the knightly vows and living by the rules of the order. If the knights were going to regain their glory days then discipline was to be instilled in the members that had strayed since the loss of Rhodes. De Valette began by reintroducing basic rules such as banning alcohol and gambling and ensuring that knights would no longer be able to live away from their auberges. His disciplinarian approach was aimed at taking things back to the times of a strict chivalric order and the three monastic vows of chastity, obedience and poverty.

The Great Siege

'Nothing is better known than the siege of Malta'
Voltaire

The knights continued their corsairing activities in the Mediterranean, capturing so many Turkish ships and causing such disruption that it was only a matter of time before the Ottoman leadership had to move on the source of the problem which was Malta. Grand Master de Valette kept his ear to the ground through an extensive espionage network that suggested an attack on the islands was being planned for mid 1565, so de Valette set about his preparations. He instructed all knights around Europe to be ready to return to Malta, organised fighting men to join them from Italy and re-strengthened the three forts. All crops and sources of food of which invading forces could have made use were to be brought within city walls, with wells and springs being made temporarily unusable. Those Maltese people not fit for or of the right age to join in the fight were moved to Sicily for the duration while the ones remaining on the island stocked up with enough provisions for a long siege and waited.

The Siege of Malta, 1565. The Arrival of the Turkish Fleet Matteo Perez d'Aleccio. (1547-1616)

Grand Master Jean Parisot de Valette gathered together the Knights of St John for a General Chapter assembly. He, more than any other present, would have known what was at stake and that many of the men facing him would lose their lives over the next few weeks. These words are recorded from that gathering;

'It is the great battle of the cross and the Koran, which is now to be fought. A formidable army of infidels are at a point of investing our island. We, for our part, are the chosen soldiers of the cross, and if Heaven requires the sacrifice of our lives, there can be no better

occasion than this. Let us hasten then my brothers to the sacred altar. There we will renew our vows and obtain, by our Faith in the Sacred Sacraments, that contempt for death which alone can render us invincible.' (Bradford, Ernie, *The Great Siege: 1565*, pg 56)

On 18th May 1565, the Ottoman fleet of Suleiman the Magnificent, under the command of his son-in-law Piali Pasha, arrived around Malta and having sailed back and forth across the south coast entered the south eastern harbour of Marsaxlokk the following day. This was something of an unexpected choice of location being so far from either the knights' base around the Grand Harbour, or the other population centre in Mdina. The chronicler Francesco Balbi di Correggio recorded the size of the Turkish fleet to be up to 200 ships and 28,000 troops with 6,300 of these being the elite Janissary forces, whilst the Knights of St John had only 6,100 troops of which 500 were knights.

The Ottoman ground forces, led by Mustapha Pasha, headed northwest across the 10 kilometres to the Sceberras Peninsular, the position of the present day Valletta. Here they set up defences against attack from the forts of St Michael and St Angelo standing over the water to the south and constructed a gunnery platform from which on 25th May, they began bombarding Fort St Elmo at the head of the peninsula. The attack was reinforced with the arrival of the corsair Dragut with 15 ships and 2,500 North African troops who were hoping for a speedy victory over the fort where de Valette, having predicted this early ground assault, had placed half of his heavy artillery capability. The fort, having constant support from Birgu and Fort St Angelo across the bay, was able to evacuate the wounded and take in new manpower and supplies, so continuing the fight for longer than the Ottoman leaders had predicted. This began to affect morale but it had nowhere near the effect of the loss of firstly the leading Janissary officer and then Dragut, one of their major strategic tacticians. Eventually Piali Pasha managed to get his ships into position to cut off St Elmo's marine supply route thus bringing an inevitable end to the fort's brave resistance. On the 23rd June it surrendered to the Turks, who proceeded to kill around 1,500 defenders left in the rubble.

The Siege of Malta, 1565. The Capture of Fort Elmo Matteo Perez d'Aleccio. (1547-1616)

The victory over Fort St Elmo came at a heavy price for both sides whilst allowing Turkish ships to safely enter Marsamxett bay from where they could constantly supply the forces on the Sceberras Peninsular and run raiding parties around to attack the other forts, Birgu and Isla. The Ottoman forces eventually surrounded the whole of Birgu and Senglea with 65 siege cannon and in an amazing and unprecedented continuous onslaught, hit the towns and forts with up to 130,000 cannonballs. By the second half of August the knights and islanders were still holding out in the blazing sun until on 6th September the Christians received the boost they had been waiting for.

The Viceroy of Sicily, Don Garcia de Toledo arrived with relief forces of 28 ships and 10,000 fighting men. They landed at Armier at the north of the island and continued onto Mdina whilst the Ottoman army, retreating from their front line positions, turned to fight de Toledo's fresh Spanish forces and others from Mdina. The resulting conflict turned into a total massacre of the Muslim army that was pushed back into St Paul's bay. The few hundred soldiers left standing sailed away from Malta, a defeated force.

The Knights of St John had faced an invasion of massively superior numbers, a four month siege and a massive bombardment of its headquarters yet had emerged victorious. The order and in particular de Valette, were the heroes of Christendom and they received gifts from throughout Europe, including a papal offer of a position as Cardinal, which he refused. The celebrated Grand Master had other plans that were going to require all the cash gifts he could attract, he wanted a new grand capital city and base for his beloved knights and to this effect the foundation stone of 'Valletta' was laid on mount Sceberras on 24th March 1566. Work on the new city was swift as the order was not sure at this point whether another attack would be forthcoming from the Ottoman Empire, but although de Valette may have eagerly watched its progress, he would not witness the order moving into its new home in 1574 as he passed away on 21st August 1568.

Rising into the Seventeenth Century

As the second half of the 16th century drew on, Malta, with its fortifications destroyed during the Great Siege of 1565 remained vulnerable to Muslim attack, so it was to this effect and the fact that the Knights of St John were now the heroes of Christendom, that King Philip of Spain garrisoned a protection force of 15,000 soldiers on the island. This provided the new Grand Master, Pierre de Monte (GM 1568-1572) with a free hand to continue the construction of the new city of Valletta with the able assistance of the Maltese architect Gerolamo Cassar.

Auberge de Castille

The order was to be moved to Valletta where a new grandiose building was to be constructed as head quarters for each langue (language) section, with surrounding accommodation for the knights and other members. The heads of the langues, with the title Pilier as they were known, would run their section with an extra particular responsibility, for example the French Pilier would also be the Grand Hospitaller, whilst the Provençal Pilier would be the Grand Preceptor (treasurer), the Castilian – Grand Chancellor, Italian – Grand Admiral, English – Grand Turcopole (mounted archers) and so on.

Grand Master Hugues Loubenx de Verdalle (GM 1581-1595)

At this time the Knights were actively corsairing and causing mayhem for Muslim shipping, confiscating goods and generally disrupting activates in the Mediterranean shipping lanes. Conflict with Ottoman forces was always a possibility during the final days of Grand Master de Monte's office. At the 1571 Battle of Lepanto the Knights of St John took part in a joint Christian conflict with the principle Ottoman fleet, decisively defeating them in the Gulf of Corinth in a clash that was to usher in a time of change. From this point on, the Ottoman Empire mainly concentrated their activities on the Eastern Mediterranean, leaving the Knights to not much more than a policing role to the west. By the early 1580s, conflict between the joint protestant British and Dutch crowns with Catholic Spain further moved the centre of military activities out of the Mediterranean and into the North Atlantic, reducing the role of the Knights even more.

Verdala Palace

After a long and distinguished career Knight John de la Cassiere took the position of Grand Master (1572-1581) after a voting stalemate position arose between two candidates that could not be resolved. With reduced military duties he was the first leader of the order that could concentrate the largest proportion of his activities on domestic affairs and he commissioned Gerolamo Cassar to design the Grand Masters Palace and a huge infirmary both of which were constructed in Valetta. It was also during de la Cassiere's period of office that an Inquisitor took up residence, beginning a time of conflicting relationships between this office and that of the Grand Master.

Grand Master Alof de Wignacourt (GM 1601-1622)
Musée de l'Armée, Paris

Maybe it was the onset of this period of relative peace and an indecisive role for the order that set the stage for a totally different type of Grand Master in Hugues Loubenx de Verdalle (GM 1581-1595). Being the preferred candidate of the Pope, the holy office took a close interest in de Verdalle's career, probably finding a friendly face in the office extremely useful politically. De Verdalle accepted the Papal offer of the position of Cardinal and Prince of the Church, the same office that Grand Master Jean Parisot de Valette had turned down after the Great Siege (probably recalling the wise adage that 'A man cannot serve two masters'). De Verdall was ostentatious in the extreme and revelled in riches, finery and the general high living with which he surrounded himself and deciding that he needed a country retreat, he had the magnificent Verdala Palace constructed on a remote hill near Dingli. In some ways symbolically, this splendid building that can be seen for miles around and is still used by the President of Malta as a summer residence, was constructed on the site of de Valette's humble shooting lodge.

The 17th century was brought in by a Grand Master who is remembered as an extremely important leader and a man of his time. Alof de Wignacourt (GM 1601-1622) recognised that a rot was developing through the excessively materialistic leadership of an Order whose very existence was supposed to be characterised by the three chivalric laws of poverty, chastity and obedience. Whilst aiming to rebuild a moral structure to the Order, de Wignacourt used his relatively peaceful times in rebuilding the navy and the infrastructure of the islands. By this time the majority of the population of Malta had migrated from the ancient capital of Mdina, which was rich in water, to Valletta, which was not and so through a master plan of engineering by the architect Bontadino dei Botnadini involving underground pipes and over ground aqueducts, this vital supply was transferred from the heights of the old city to the new. Part of the vast cost of this operation was covered by the Grand Master himself, who was also responsible for resupplying the island with food at a time of shortage by the taking of two Turkish galleys filled with grain. De Wignacourt also financed all but one of six small defensive coastal forts he had constructed in strategic positions, five of which still remain standing and which became the beginning of a chain of such defensive towers added to by the future Grand Masters Giovanni Paolo Lascaris and Martin de Redin.

Wignacourt Aqueduct, Santa Venera

The ongoing corsairing raids on shipping from North Africa and the land raiding parties that the Order continued throughout the 17th Century, significantly included the attack on the Greek city of Corinth in 1611, where they left it sacked and pillaged. In 1614 it appeared that Malta was to experience the force of another backlash when 60 galleys appeared in the waters off Marsaxlokk, where the population was quickly removed to a place of safety whilst the knights very easily saw the intruders off. The Turkish fleet showed its hand again in 1669 when they invaded and captured Candia, Crete, inspiring Grand Master Nicolas Cotoner (GM 1663-1680) to embark on a massive engineering project in Malta to fortify Birgu, Isla and Bormla, the results of which can still be seen in the huge inland wall that protects the 'Three Cities' today.

The navy once again had a great reputation under de Wignacourt and the Order in general was more accepted by the population as being on their side. After these last skirmishes more peaceful times developed and the Knights concentrated further on their administrational role as leaders of Malta under the oversight of the Grand Master whose office since 1607 had been invested with the added title of 'Prince of the Holy Roman Empire'.

De Wignacourt appeared to have understood the value of the historical times in which he lived and that the Order was creating and noticed that many of their official documents, manuscripts and books were being disposed of outside the Order. To remedy this situation he passed a statute in 1612 declaring that all such material must be preserved until an appropriate library could be set up although it wasn't until 1650 that Grand Master Giovanni Lascaris set up such a facility in the vestry of St John's church. In keeping with de Wignacourt's appreciation of art and literature, he supported the attempts of the painter Caravaggio to join the Knights of St John by having him accepted into the Order as a Knight of Obedience after his arrival from Italy in 1608. In fact the great artist was anything but obedient and soon found himself imprisoned after a fight with a senior knight and after somehow escaping from Fort St Angelo, he fled to Sicily and was defrocked in his absence. Three of Caravaggio's works in particular can be recognised as associated with his time as a Knight, two portraits of his Grand Master and patron, Alof de Wignacourt and his masterpiece, 'The Beheading of St John'.

After his death in 1622 on a hunting expedition, de Wignacourt was remembered as a great leader and a Grand Master who brought wealth and prosperity to the Order, whilst setting the stage for a different age for them. The C17th Baroque style of opulent extravagance in architecture, design and art coming from Rome and fostered by the Church, was whole-heartily taken up by the Order and it began to be reflected in their buildings and decoration. In the more peaceful times that characterized the 17th century, the people of Malta and Gozo lived as if in a relatively wealthy kingdom under their Royal institution; Knights of St John and its various Grand Masters.

Declining into the Eighteenth Century

The turning of the 18th Century was overseen by the new Grand Master Ramon Perellos de Rocaful (gm 1697-1720) who, like his predecessor de Wignacourt, loved the arts but whilst he actively encouraged their development on the island he was also a pragmatic leader and was well aware that he had to face up to the times as he found them. The turning of world events, with not a little help from the Knights, meant that the Maltese population were now enjoying easier times being secure both financially and militarily. With this situation well and truly in mind Perellos was determined to remain neutral in international affairs in keeping with its multinational status. To this effect an alliance with Russia, against Turkey offered in 1698, was turned down. The winds of change though had left the Order of St John somewhat without a raison d'etre and they were searching for a role to take then forward into the 18th Century.

Porte des Bombes

As with so many previous grand masters Perellos saw the renovation of the navy as being the key to breathing of new life into the Order, the fleet had become worn down and out of date so he commenced on a massive campaign to build new ships, even going as far as financing the first one himself. Being for ever pragmatic the construction of larger more efficient navy had the added benefit of allowing for a smaller and less cash hungry fleet. Finding enemies to fight though, was not as easy as it had been as the Turks were actively trading with European states, greatly reducing the age old practice of raiding their ships, so the Knights were forced to confine most of their coirsaring activates to the Barbary States of North Africa. Perellos's new fleet did successfully carry out raids, brining in much needed revenue and in commemoration he had the fine baroque 'Porte des Bombes' archway built into the external wall fortifications of the new town of Floriana (The Floriana Lines). Unfortunately Perellos did not live to see its completion in 1721, but it stands in memory of him as do the many fine tapestries he had erected in the Grand Master Palace and in St John Cathedral, where his funerary monument is a fine example of the Baroque.

Grand Master António Manoel de Vilhena (gm 1722-1736)

The mantle was carried forward by Grand Master António Manoel de Vilhena (gm 1722-1736), and 'Manoel', as he became popularly known, followed very much in the footsteps of his predecessor in combining actions to assist the islands population with keeping the Knights occupied. By this time Malta had become a desirable place to live and with a population of around 100,000 squashing into the narrow streets of Valletta the new town of Floriana was built to take the strain. This extension to the capitol city was named after the Italian architect Pietro Paolo Floriani who designed the fortification line around the area, to include Perellos's Porte des Bombes. Manoel instructed various humanitarian building projects within Floriana and Valletta in keeping with the Order's history including a women's hospital and a hospital for incurables and also a theatre in 1731. In a further attempt to bridge any remaining gap between the islanders and the Order, new buildings were constructed for the islands Università, the islands old governmental body, both in Mdina and Victoria, Gozo, a move which also had the effect of strengthening central control of the Knights of St John as an upper sovereign body.

Whilst efforts to consolidate peaceful relations with the populace was taking effect the problem still lay before the Grand Master of how to bring the knights themselves into the 18th century and to end their gambling and the competition between the langues, that was resulting in duelling. In searching for an occupation for the knights Manoel turned to the brand new naval fleet that had been supplied through the efforts of Grand Master Perellos and which meant that he could meet any opponent on at least an equal footing. To lead the way in 1723 he promoted Perellos's Lieutenant of the Galleys, Chevalier Jacques Chambray, to Captain of the San Vincenzo in which he fought over 30 battles and took 53 enemy ships captive, his valour and ruddy complexion winning him the nick-name 'Le Rouge De Malte' with his enemies.

It may be seen as a somewhat ironic sign of the times that one of Manoel's greatest achievements, the construction of a magnificent fort on a small island in Marsamxett harbour and which took his name, never found a use as the Turks, now eager to trade with the West, had no use for war or invasion. It could be regarded as remarkable epitaph of peace left to the island by a Grand Master who inspired much respect and affection from all sections of the people in Malta when he past away in 1736.

Grand Master Manoel Pinto de Fonseca (gm 1741-1773)
Musée de l'Armée, Paris

Manoel de Vilhena's name sake and former chancellor, Grand Master Manoel Pinto de Fonseca (gm 1741-1773) did not attract the epitaph of 'man of his times', in fact overlooking many of the financial and political pressures facing the Order, he harked back to times of pomp and grandeur. A position that for a leader who was to be in office for 32 years, the longest of any Grand Master, at such a vital point in their history may have proved crucial to their future survival in Malta. In a positive measure Pinto attempted to introduce silk manufacture to the islands whilst sending the economy in a downward spiral by increasing taxation and borrowing heavily for building projects such as the university that opened in 1769. At the same time relationships with the King of France, an old supporter and ally of the Order, was becoming strained as the French palace was concentrating on trading relations with the Ottormans, so much that the king ordered the release of the Mustapha Pasha after a failed plot to assassinate the Grand Master and take the over Malta. Pinto released Pasha without objecting as he had was laying his own clandestine and eventually doomed plot to annex the island of Corsica.

It appears that Pinto was more obsessed with the power of his office than others were and this may have been his Achilles Heal, maybe a little more humility might have provided a clearer view of the vastly changing European political and economic scene. The vast financial pressures that engulfed Pinto's time in office may have been better confronted through a unified front involving the whole population of the Maltese islands, but instead he alienated the islands aristocracy by removing ancient rights and the other islanders through a heavy burden of taxation. For all this Pinto was not well remembered after he died at the fully ripened age of 92, which in itself courted quiet suspicion as it was known that the alchemist Count Cagliostro had lodged with him for some time whilst working on an elixir of longevity.

Loss of Malta and French Occupation

On taking over as Grand Master, Francesco Ximenes de Texada (gm 1773-1775), faced an economy in decline a treasury in disarray and economic systems left in turmoil by Pinto de Fonseca's previous administration. It could be seen as somewhat ironic under these circumstances that one of his earliest decisions was to move the government pawnbrokers into new smart accommodation in Valletta, probably in an attempt to gain much needed revenue from the suffering islanders. In equally bottom up policies Ximenes lowered the wages of government employees and banned the hunting of rabbits in a clumsy attempt to restock the islands supply of livestock. Then in September 1775 the people of Malta having taken enough austerity at the hands of the Grand Master took part in an unsuccessful revolt where Ximenes was supposed to have been assassinated. In an attempt to quell the storm Ximenes promised to reinstate the rights he had taken from the people and to let the ring leaders of the insurrection go free but after a few days had them put to death and their heads displayed in public. This outright betrayal of the people brought about massive unrest that could have removed the Knights of Malta from power if it wasn't for the death of Ximenes and the reassuring attitude of the knights in general.

Grand Master, Francesco Ximenes de Texada (gm 1773-1775)

With a temporary reprieve at home European politics was playing its own game and for the Knights the rules were changing. It was during the time of the French Grand Master Emmanuel de Rohan-Polduc (gm 1775-1797), that the French Revolution (1787-1789) shook the world of the aristocracy and Orthodox Church in the country that supplied the majority of knights to the order and income from its properties. In August 1792 the Tuileries Palace, the royal residence in Paris, was attacked and King Louis XVI was captured, dethroned and imprisoned in the Temple, the home of the French Grand Master. The following month in a devastating move for the Order, all their French properties were confiscated by the state, greatly escalating the financial problems of Rohan-Polduc. King Louis and his queen Marie Antoinette were beheaded in January 1793, four years before the death of their great friend Rohan-Polduc, who had proved throughout his 22 years in office to be a humane and just leader with an impossible task to perform.

As the European political game developed in the second half of the eighteenth century, Russia became the emerging power on the board and whilst this entity was mistrusted and avoided by Rohan-Polduc its presence was growing in the Mediterranean. Russian sea trade in the area meant that contact with Malta was inevitable and as time past trust and cooperation developed between the two parties.

Grand Master Ferdinand von Hompesch (gm 1797-1798)

With the process of the partition of Poland beginning in 1793, much of the properties of the Polish Langue past over to Russian control, producing a threat to the revenues from these estates, so with political relations becoming increasingly important to Malta by 1795 they had ambassadors embedded in Russia. Then with the death of Catherine 'The Great' of Russia, in 1796 the Order found a friend and supporter in her successor Czar Paul I (r 1776-1801), who being of a

Conservative persuasion saw the chivalric order as the arbiters of the highest standards of aristocracy. In keeping with this development the Order's Polish organisation was changed to become the Russian Grand Priory, with control over 10 commanderies and then under Grand Master Ferdinand von Hompesch (gm 1797-1798), Paul was made the new protector of the order in August 1797.

The success of the French revolution led to it moving beyond the countries boarders and spreading across Europe including Germany, the home of many of the Order's properties and importantly, Britain. In 1796 Napoleon Bonaparte was promoted Brigadier general and became leader of the French army in Italy from where he laid plans to incorporate India into his empire. To achieve this he knew he would need a foot hold in Egypt and some control of the Mediterranean, where he hoped to avoid Nelson's mighty British Navy as much as possible. The one aspect that has driven so much of Malta's history is its strategic position and this had now become important to Bonaparte's plans and he arrived in Maltese waters on 9th June 1798 with 30,000 men, on route for Egypt. On receiving a request from Bonaparte for permission to enter the Grand Harbour to take on provisions von Hompesch replied that as a neutral state they would only allow four ships to entre at once. This predictable reply was enough to provide Bonaparte with an excuse to attack the island and on 11th June the French landed at various coastal points, sending the Knights of St John into disarray, if not desertion, leaving a couple of thousand local militia to hold off for around two days. The French firstly took Mdina and then agreed a surrender of Valetta and the rest of the islands with von Hompesch signing the agreement onboard the flagship, the L'Orient. Why von Hompesch gave up the island without a fight when Valletta was strongly defended we can only speculate, but with the island thus secured, Bonaparte left 4,000 men and carried on to Alexandria on 19th June. A more unceremonial and pitifully sad end to 268 years of Malta's fascinating history and its association with the Knight's of St John could not be imagined.

Capitulation of Malta to General Bonaparte
Gottfried-Baumann

It was agreed that von Hompesch would receive a pension of 300,000 franks, although he probably saw nothing of this and that he would to leave the island with any other active knights within three weeks. He head off to Trieste in Italy, whilst others went to St Petersburgh in Russia, looking for the protection of Czar Paul I (gm 1798-1801) who became Grand

Master on 27th October 1798. This was a strange choice for a leader of a monastic, Catholic order as he was not a Catholic and was married and also von Hompesch was officially still in post until he abdicated on 6th July 1799.

If the populace of Malta had been in two minds about the arrival of French troops on the island any uncertainty soon disappeared when the occupying armies began to loot churches and private property, accumulating a huge fortune in booty, ostensibly to pay for Bonaparte's campaign in Egypt. On top of this the younger Maltese men were being press ganged to join the French forces. The public response was almost unanimous outrage and the people took to the streets en-masse forcing the French out of Mdina and the countryside, confining them in Valletta and the Three Cities area. It took two years and the help of the British, for the French to surrender on 5th September 1800, when it was agreed that the islands would be put under the protection of the British.

A Modern Order of St John

Czar Paul was extremely unpopular with the Russian nobility and had only served as Grand Master for three years when he was assassinated in his bed chamber after refusing to sign a document announcing his abdication. Paul's son, Alexander was present at St Michael's Palace in St Petersburg, when the incident took place and may well have been aware of the conspiracy that elevated him to the position of Emperor of Russia at the age of 23. It is probable that Alexander knew of the attempt to dethrone his father but his death was not expected and it is said that it led to him suffering from terrible guilt and remorse throughout his remaining days.

Czar Paul I of Russia (gm 1798-1801)

As the Order was not in a position to carry out its obligations and activities it was thought that the Grand Mastership should be temporarily be put on hold with interim Lieutenants filing the role and to this effect Count Nicolai Saltykov (lieu 1801-1803), was appointed.

Czar Alexander had no interest in taking over the role of Grand Master of the Knights of St John but being a practical man and knowing the strategic value of the Maltese Islands, he agreed to put the Knights under his imperial protection and promised to have their status and position on Malta reinstated. This return to the Order's island home must have appeared imminent after the Treaty of Amiens (1802) ordered just such a move to be made within three months. The islanders though had no intension of going down that road again and the peace that the treaty provided between France, England, Spain and the other parties affected by the Napoleonic War, only lasted 14 months. Another idea that was discussed between various national leaders in the search for a future for the Order was to combine them with the Tutonic Knights but this also did not come to fruition.

With the possibility of the Order regaining occupation of Malta still on the table after the Treaty of Amiens, the appointment of Bartolomeo Ruspoli as Grand Master by Pope Pius VII, on 16th September 1802, again fell on stony ground as Ruspoli had studied the political situation and turned down the position. This must have appeared to be the last opportunity of regaining the status quo for the Order and to this end Giovanni Battista Tommasi (GM 1803-1805), took the job and positioned a base in Messina. Tommasi's hope of using this Sicilian foothold to organise a short sea crossing over to Malta in order to regain control of the island, was purposely interrupted by the British Commander Alexander Ball who persuaded the Grand Master that he would be met by an extremely unwelcoming local populace.

In June 1805, after a long and fruitless campaign to regain his Grand Mastership, Ferdinand von Hompesch died impoverished in Montpellier. By this time the Order was in an extremely poor state with not only the three English and the Spanish langues having been taken under crown control but also the Northern Italian properties all sequestered and the Russian Priory dissolved. With the death of Tommasi, in Catania, on 13th June 1805, the Grand Mastership was again suspended with the appointment as Lieutenant of Innico Maria Guevara-Suardo (lieu 1805-1814).

After a few years of relative inactivity, in 1827 the Order took on new head quarters in Ferrara, Northern Italy, under Lieutenant Antonio Busca (lieu 1821-1834), in a move that could be seen as the beginning of a way forward into a future function for the Knights. Then in 1831 with a move to Rome they took over the Palazzo Malta, on the Via Condotti, the former residence of the Order's ambassador to the Vatican, where they remain today. With a return to the early focus on running hospitals supported by charitable activities the Order took on a new structure made up of various National Associations that took the place of the old langues. In 1855 the female order of the Sisters of St John of Jerusalem was inaugurated and in 1866, during the Austro-Prussian War, the Order opened its first military hospital in Vienna. Then, in a historical move that would have appeared impossible only a few years earlier, in 1876 the Order of St John opened a hospital in Tantur, south of Jerusalem, 600 years after it first began its activities in the Holy Lands. It was then only three years until the line of Grand Masters recommenced with Giovanni Battista Ceschi a Santa Croce, (GM 1879-1905).

The British began a section of the order in 1831 that was not recognised by the central body in Rome, so going it alone, they introduced the 'Grand Priory of the Order of the Hospital of St John of Jerusalem in the British Realm', followed in 1877 by the first St John's Ambulance Association that is still going strong today.

During the First and Second World Wars the order acted under its sovereign independent status to bring medical relief to the wounded and then with the onset of peace the 'Johannite-Unfall-Hilfe', or Ambulance Service was founded in

1945. The Order was then granted observer status at the United Nations in 1988, under the British Grand Master Andrew Willoughby Bertie, (GM 1988-2008).

Today the Order is led by another Britain, Matthew Festing, who after serving as the Grand Prior of England became Grand Master on 11th March 2008 and remains in the position in 2015, at the time of writing. The Grand Master has the Status of Cardinal of the Roman Catholic Church, Prince of the Holy Roman Empire, Royal Prince of Rhodes and Malta and is recognised internationally as a head of state.

Originally known as the 'Knights Hospitallers', or the 'Knights of St John of Jerusalem', the Order has altered its name over the years as circumstances and situations changed. The proper title now is the 'Sovereign Military Hospitaller Order of St John of Jerusalem of Rhodes and of Malta'. It is also known as the 'Sovereign Military Order of Malta' and the 'Knights of Malta', although many versions of the name have been legally registered throughout the World.

Chapter 5

The British
(1800 – 1964)

Napoleonic Conflict and British Relief

The reason for the early capitulation of the Knight's of St John as the ruling power of the Maltese islands with the arrival of Napoleon's fleet is a matter of conjecture but what is certain is that the Order left in a state of turmoil and disarray, leaving the islands in the control of the French in June 1798. It was not long before the behaviour of the occupying forces led to serious conflict with the Maltese populace who after forming a militia, forced the French out of Mdina and the countryside and confined them in the Valletta and Three Cities areas. As this state of semi-imprisonment was, as far as the Maltese could take the situation, without reinforcement and supplies, they looked towards the British and king Ferdinand of Sicily for help in expelling the French from the islands.

At the time, Nelson and the British fleet were pre-occupied with Napoleon further east in the Mediterranean where the French were thoroughly routed at the Battle of the Nile in the heat of August 1798, with Napoleon loosing most of his fleet together with his flagship L 'Orient. Nelson was nursing his battered navy home when he encountered a small vessel hailing him off the coast of Sicily and when it came aside his flagship Vanguard he met with the two Maltese delegates, Luigi Briffa and Francesco Farrugia who presented the Admiral with a letter from their National Assembly asking for his assistance. In truth the Maltese had no idea of the whereabouts of the British fleet and this was a totally chance encounter and one that was to introduce a whole new chapter into the history of their islands. Nelson was sympathetic to the plight of the Maltese and immediately arranged for the Portuguese to affect a blockage off Malta until he could organise a more thorough British response. This began with the arrival of the 74 gun HMS Orion with Captain James Saumarez, Nelson's second in command at the Battle of the Nile, at the helm. He was followed by Captain Alexander Ball in HMS Alexander, Captain Manley Dixon in HMS Lion and Captain George Baker in the fireship HMS Incendiary. By 12th October the island was safely surrounded and ready for Admiral Nelson to arrive to assess the situation, which he did on 26th October. A couple of days later Captain Alexander Ball and Marine Captain John Creswell landed on Gozo and after taking control of Fort Chambray, secured the island.

With the coming of the New Year of 1799, the French were still ensconced in Malta's capital when Nelson, in a move that shocked the islanders, allowed the Portuguese to depart the scene leaving only the British and in a panic response a contingent of Maltese took part in a failed attempt to penetrate and take back Valletta. The wider picture in the Mediterranean was also cause for concern as Napoleon, having taken Naples, was turning his eyes to Sicily, which was vital for Maltese food supplies. Seeing a bleak future, a Maltese delegation approached Nelson and requested that the islands be put under British protection. The admiral readily agreed and went into action by bringing in four ships of war to strengthen the blockade and, after due consultation with King Ferdinand of Naples, appointed Captain Ball (cc 1799-1801) as the first 'Civil Commissioner' of Malta. He also moved in two regiments under the command of Brigadier-General Thomas Gordon that arrived off Malta on 9th December on board the ships HMS Northumberland and Culloden and ferried over 1,200 Russian troops from Sicily. The combined forces gathered to assist the British remove the French were still short in number so the Maltese Light Infantry was founded in June 1800.

The blockade of Valletta was having an effect as food supplies were getting short, so much so that the Maltese population were forced out of the city reducing its number from the usual 45,000 down to below 10,000 hungry mouths. Even though the shortages were causing illness and a deadly typhus epidemic was increasing pressure, the word from the French General, Claude-Henri de Vaubois, within Valletta was "Keen to deserve the esteem of your nation, as you seek that of ours, we are resolved to defend this fortress until the end" and "This place is in too good a situation, and I am too conscious of the service of my country and my honour, to listen to your proposals".

As the summer of 1800 drew on, the situation in Valletta got steadily worse until the point where up to 100 men were dying every day and all the dogs, cats and rabbits had been eaten and even the horses had been boiled for soup. Two French ships made a run through the blockade using the cover of the extra dark night of 24th August and whilst the 'Diane', under Captain Solen, was captured, Captain Jean Villeneuve manoeuvred the 'Justice' through the British line and escaped to Toulon. This turned out to be a final dash for freedom as on the 4th September the British General Pigot received envoys from Vaubois who accepted the total and absolute surrender terms of handing over the island and everything on it to the British. With the French leaving the islands after holding out for two years, Malta was now a British Protectorate and Captain Alexander Ball was driven into Valletta as the first 'Civil Commissioner', to the cheering of the gathered masses and with the Union Jack flying on all public buildings.

Captain Alexander Ball

From Protectorate to Colony

British control of the Maltese Islands must have seemed like a win-win situation with the Maltese people looking towards a future of peaceful and fair leadership combined with protection from potential invaders. The British had received an ideally situated island sitting strategically in the only narrow point of the shipping lanes of the Mediterranean, sought after by many powers throughout history since the Phoenicians landed on Malta 1,100 years earlier. The island now had been developed through 268 years serving as the base for the Knights of St John, with harbours, docks, warehouses and official buildings all ready for use.

The Evacuation of Malta (1803)
Cartoon by James Gillray (1756-1815)

The first item on the British agenda was to restore effective processes of administration after the turmoil of the last few of years and for this they brought in Charles Cameron (cc 1801-1802), to replace Ball as Civil Commissioner, who ensured that courts, hospitals and all civil amenities were running effectively and that tax, customs revenues were being collected. As life on Malta appeared to be getting back to normality, problems were lurking in the background that were going to have to be dealt with, for one thing the islands were legally still under the sovereign ownership of Sicily and another was Czar Paul of Russia, who being made Grand Master of the Order of St John, had kept them together until he was assassinated in 1801 and they would be looking at restoring the islands to the Order. The Maltese had no wish to see either the reinstatement of the Knights, especially as they had become insolvent after the loss of most of their oversees property, or the French who they had recently driven off the island. To this end a delegation of representatives from the Maltese villages visited Commissioner Cameron on 19th October 1801, to request that Britain remain in control of Malta and on being told that this decision was beyond his scope of authority, they set off for an audience with the government, arriving in London on 1st February 1802. To confirm the intent and wishes of the Maltese people they prepared and presented, in June 1802, the document 'The Declaration of Rights of the inhabitants of the Islands of Malta and Gozo', (La Dichiarazione dei Diritti degli abitanti delle Isole di Malta e Gozo), it was signed by 104 senior representatives from across the island and proclaimed that George III was their king and that he was obliged not to surrender the islands to any other power and that they should be allowed self governance whilst as a 'British Protectorate'.

Britain was also still engaged in the French Revolutionary War which meant political uncertainty throughout Europe and it was to confront this that the Treaty of Amiens was signed on 25th March 1802, which whilst bringing peace between Britain and France, also held that Malta should be returned to the Knights of St John within three months. The end to hostilities was of course a sound development but the prospect of losing Malta was thoroughly unpopular with the British people, the press and with parliament. In reality the Treaty did not appear to have a great deal of an effect in hearts and minds of either side and it soon became clear that the return of the Knights would now be tantamount to a reinstatement of the French control of Malta. As complex circumstances can change quickly in European politics, especially at times of conflict, the British Government appeared to react to events firstly with stalling tactics and then with a clear decision to go against the Treaty and to keep control of Malta.

The recently reinstated, now Rear-Admiral Sir Alexander Ball (cc 1802-1809), received instructions from London on 17th October 1802 to end plans to leave Malta and to continue to act in his role as Civil-Commissioner. Whilst the disagreements between the parties were much more complicated than can be covered here, Malta became an important point of ultimatum and Napoleon Bonaparte's reaction to Britain's change of heart was to leave Malta or go to war. Britain had no intention of abandoning Malta so the Napoleonic Wars (1803-1915), commenced on 18th May 1803.

Under the war years the Maltese islands found wealth through utilizing its position in the Mediterranean and acting as a centre for shipping and sea trade but by the end of the conflict in 1809 it was clear that a decision was going to have to be reached about their future status. It was the turn of Civil-Commissioner, Lieutenant-General Sir Hildebrand Oakes (cc 1810-1813), to play his part when he headed a commission that was to report back to London on the state of the islands and its population in all things except military matters, in a step toward colonization. It was felt that by this time Malta had become wealthy under the protection of Britain and that as such the islands were now an important part of Britain's international economic position. On 20th June 1812, the two other members of the commission William A Cout and John Burrows arrived in Malta. With fortuitous timing Russia's alliance with France was dissolved with the Czar now siding with Britain, a situation that led to an abandonment of any claim on Malta by their new partners on behalf of the Order of St John.

Malta was becoming increasingly wealthy and political events were moving forward at a pace when disaster struck in March 1813 with the arrival, in the Grand Harbour, of a merchant ship from Alexandria that brought with it the bubonic plague. The disease spread through Valletta like wild fire, then throughout the island and across to Gozo by January 1814. The new British leader, Lieutenant-General Sir Thomas Maitland (gov 1813-1824), the first to have the title Governor, arrived on 4th October 1813, in the middle of the epidemic and with past knowledge of such a situation he immediately put into action various isolation measures. By this time the disease may have peaked and the island was declared clear of the plague in March 1814 after it had taken 4,486 lives, around 4% of the population.

Maitland took up his position as Governor under the so called 'Bathurst Constitution', that effectively made Malta a British colony, but it was not actually a constitution being merely a statement of instruction from Lord Bathurst, Secretary of State for the Colonies in London, which was basically;

'The authority of the Governor is limited only by word of the King, he is responsible to His Majesty and to his country for his conduct, but his discretion is not to be shackled by any body of persons resident in Malta', also *'Free exorcise of religious worship to all persons who inhabit or frequent the islands'.* (Rudolf, Uwe Jens, & Berg, Warren, *Historical Dictionary of Malta*, Pg 38).

The Bathurst Constitution gained further validity at the signing of the Treaty of Paris on 30th May 1814, that marked the defeat of France by the sixth Coalition of countries, (Britain, Austria, Prussia, Russia, Portugal, Sweden, Spain, Germany), as part of the Napoleonic Wars. Under the treaty it was held that Great Britain was to keep sovereignty over the island of Malta therefore formally recognising it as a Crown Colony. This was then set in stone at the 'Congress of Vienna', one of the most fundamental and historic European conferences, held between September 1814 and June 1815 to reshape Europe after the defeat of Napoleon.

Life in Maltese Britain

Malta's first decade as a British colony was dominated by Governor and Commander-in-Chief, Thomas Maitland, who had been given the task of formulating effective Civil Administration for the islands. Maitland's nick name of 'King Tom' came from his approach that from the beginning was one of authoritarian control that left no one in doubt of who was in charge whilst remaining sympathetic to the views and expectations of the islanders. One of his first tasks was to appoint a Chief Secretary to the Government, the head position and his second in charge in the task of running the new or rearranged departments of Treasury, Trade, the Office of Port Duties and Collection of Excise and a new police service modelled on the English system. Gozo had a similar system of its own, to be run along side Malta's, under its own Commander. Any hopes of Maltese involvement in the higher positions of the new Civil Administration were soon dashed when it became clear that all theses jobs were to be given to Englishmen. An attempt was made though, to appease Maltese nobles, by making six of them Lord-Lieutenants of various areas of Malta, positions that would play to the ego of the nobles but that were really only of nominal status and lacked in any real power.

As part of Maitland's new strategy for the islands he increased spending in all departments, paid for through the strict collection of port custom duties and rents on public properties. In another attempt to improve the economy he encouraged the focus on shipping and trade especially in local and British products and abolishing export duty, whilst involving trade with the far off West Indies. These efforts did have some positive influence on these islands that were still suffering the effects of the devastating plague of 1813. Ironically it was this very epidemic that was inhibiting real international trade in Malta, as the Governor did not lift the island's quarantine rules that were keeping many foreign trade ships away.

Various issues were also confronted in respect to the judicial system that were highlighted in the Royal Commission of 1812 and changes were introduced; for example to avoid corruption judges would receive a fixed salary and would be guaranteed a position for life, witnesses should no longer be interrogated in private but in open court and jury trials would be abolished as they were not thought appropriate in such a small community except in criminal cases. The power of the

Governor to reverse court decisions was abolished and torture, corsairing and slavery were to be made highly illegal.

A close relationship between the island's leaders and the Roman Church was a legacy from the times of the Catholic, Knights of St John that was causing tension between the island's religious leaders and Maitland's Administration. The ownership of the fine St John's Church, in Valletta was a particular point of conjecture that came to a head in 1816 when the Pope, considering it as belonging to Rome, upgraded it to the status of Co-Cathedral. Maitland, on the other hand, considered the building to be an asset of the state and was considering converting it into a Protestant Cathedral. Maybe it was the warning of Lord Bathurst not to come between the Maltese and their church that led to the compromise agreement to allow the church to remain Catholic whilst keeping it under state ownership. The previous year saw a disagreement regarding the Grandmaster's throne in the same church. Now that the Knights had left the island a decision had to be made as to who was to sit on the esteemed seat during services, the Governor or the Bishop. In a fine show of clever diplomacy he had the royal coat of arms carved onto the throne, dedicating it to the king and stating that it had to be left vacant in case his Royal Highness was ever in attendance. The Governor further attempted to reduce the power of the church by introducing a law to the effect that any properties left to the church had to be disposed of within one year, otherwise they reverted to the state, but this so called Mortmain Law of 1822, effectively died with Maitland, who passed away two years later.

The next Governor, Francis Edward Rawdon-Hastings, 1st Marquess of Hastings (gov 1824-1826), was extremely experienced having previously been Governor General of India and this new appointment may have been something of a swansong for the elderly aristocrat. Rawdon-Hastings's initial impression of Malta was one of unnecessary poverty amongst the island's working class with the result of a predominance of begging on an island that only a decade or so previously had been known for its wealthy status.

As overseas trade was the obvious way to improve the economic state of the island, Rawdon-Hastings immediately dissolved the quarantine laws that had kept shipping away and expressly encouraged trade throughout the Mediterranean. As a producer of raw cotton, Malta suddenly found a new market in Britain, where the English cotton industry was booming and where Rawdon-Hastings had organised tax-free importing of the Maltese crop. The British army and navy were instructed to actively recruit amongst the youth of Malta and emigration was encouraged, both measures being introduced in an effort to quickly relieve unemployment. Then as these measures were taking effect under Governor Sir Henry Frederick Bouverie (gov 1836-1843), Malta suffered an epidemic of cholera that took 4,253 lives out of a population of around 123,000 in 1837, the year that also saw the beginning of the Victorian era.

By this time the foundations of British rule of Malta had been laid and although the next decades saw more Governors come and go, it could be said that the wealth and health of Malta grew in line with Britain and other western countries. Over this time government officials sometimes reported of the prosperity of the islands and sometimes of their relative poverty so a true picture would be hard to draw. The truth, though, probably lies somewhere in the middle, with the aristocratic element of Maltese society having the lion's share of the wealth with the mass majority seeing little of it. It is equally difficult to find an accurate account of the day to day life on Malta considering the constant string of Western European Gentlemen and members of the Gentry visiting the islands on the 'Grand Tour'. That is apart from the wonderful imagery left to us by William Thackeray Makepeace, in his 'Notes on a Journey from Cornhill to Grand Cairo', whose descriptions of his visit to Malta began in the Grand Harbour;

'On the 5th, to the inexpressible joy of all, we reached Valletta, the entrance to the harbour of which is one of the most stately and agreeable scenes ever admired by a sea-sick traveller. The small basin was busy with a hundred ships, from the huge guard-ship, which lies there a city in itself;--merchantmen loading and crews cheering, under all the flags of the world flaunting in the sunshine; a half-score of busy black steamers perpetually coming and going, coaling and painting, and puffing and hissing in and out of harbour; slim men-of-war's barges shooting to and fro, with long shining oars flashing like wings over the water; hundreds of painted town-boats, with high heads and white awnings,--down to the little tubs in which some naked, tawny young beggars came paddling up to the steamer, entreating us to let them dive for halfpence. Round this busy blue water rise rocks, blazing in sunshine, and covered with every imaginable device of fortification; to the right, St. Elmo, with flag and lighthouse; and opposite, the Military Hospital, looking like a palace; and all round, the houses of the city, for its size the handsomest and most stately in the world'.

On arriving in Valletta he continued;

'Nor does it disappoint you on a closer inspection, as many a foreign town does. The streets are thronged with a lively comfortable-looking

population; the poor seem to inhabit handsome stone palaces, with balconies and projecting windows of heavy carved stone. The lights and shadows, the cries and stenches, the fruit-shops and fish-stalls, the dresses and chatter of all nations; the soldiers in scarlet, and women in black mantillas; the beggars, boat-men, barrels of pickled herrings and macaroni; the shovel-hatted priests and bearded capuchins; the tobacco, grapes, onions, and sunshine; the signboards, bottled-porter stores, the statues of saints and little chapels which jostle the stranger's eyes as he goes up the famous stairs from the Water-gate, make a scene of such pleasant confusion and liveliness as I have never witnessed before. And the effect of the groups of multitudinous actors in this busy cheerful drama is heightened, as it were, by the decorations of the stage. The sky is delightfully brilliant; all the houses and ornaments are stately; castle and palaces are rising all around; and the flag, towers, and walls of Fort St. Elmo look as fresh and magnificent as if they had been erected only yesterday'. (Thackeray, William Makepeace, *Notes on a Journey from Cornhill to Grand Cairo*, p,26/27.)

These hectic and lively scenes received a boost with the outbreak of the Crimean War in October 1853 with French and British warships packing into the dockyards all demanding chandlering services with the sailors and the garrisoned troops taking advantage of the shops and bars of Valletta. Malta was too far west to be directly involved with the actual theatre of war but its position as a base of operations was crucial and extremely lucrative for the islanders. The islands hospitals turned out to be vital for the wounded returning west on damaged ships that required the expertise of the Maltese and British workers.

The one thing that was driven firmly into the collective mind of the British government by the Crimean War was the vulnerability of the Maltese Islands and after the conflicts had ended it was decided that reinforcements were required. In 1866 William Francis Drummond, the Assistant Inspector of General Fortifications, was brought in to report on the situation. As a result new, state of the art, 10 inch guns were delivered from London and installed at strategic points around Valletta, Floriana and around the perimeter forts. A plan was implemented to have supporting forts built opposite each other at harbour mouths and channels and a large new one was completed in Sliema in 1877. To protect the more densely inhabited eastern section of Malta in the case of landed troops, extra forts were constructed at high points, which together with an extensive wall system, stretched across the west of the island. These so called 'Victoria Lines' were finished in 1897, the year of the Queen's Diamond Jubilee, to complete the island's most thorough fortification works since the Knights and at a cost of four million pounds.

With the outbreak of the First World War on 28th July 1914, the combined French and British forces must have been thankful that such extensive refortification works had already been carried out and that the island could easily become a safe base for the French fleet, over a hundred years since the now allied British had evacuated them from the same island. As Malta was receiving an influx of troops and the strategic gun batteries were being manned up, the Maltese requested direct involvement with the fighting and so on 14th January 1915, the first battalion of the King's Own Malta Regiment were sent to Cyprus, in the Turkish war theatre.

Governor Field-Marshal, Lord Paul Methuen (gov 1915-1919)

In the February, Governor Field-Marshal, Lord Paul Methuen (gov 1915-1919) set about turning Malta into a perfectly situated rear base whilst the first ships of the conflict were running into minefields off the Gallipoli Peninsula with a loss of four vessels. This served to highlight the need for Malta to take on its historic role as an island hospital and public buildings were converted to take on the task. This massive medical base was treating over 4,000 wounded after the April landing in Gallipoli, where the allies suffered up to 38,000 casualties after being successfully repelled by Ottoman forces. Although the front line theatre of war did not get near to Malta, one of the major threats in the Mediterranean came from the minefields that were continually hampering the allied fleet and the job of confronting this was given to the Malta Minesweeping fleet.

With the tides of war eventually turning in favour of the Allies, the Armistice was signed on 11th November 1918 by the Allied and German forces, bringing the First World War to an end to the relief of millions and the new peace brought calm to the recently dynamically active Malta. It may have been widely anticipated that the west could now expect to bask in the glory of victory and in fact an economic boom followed the end of the war but this deadly conflict had been costly and Europe soon fell into economic depression and mass unemployment. In Malta the blame was placed, by many, on the British Administration when in fact people all over Europe were experiencing the economic downfall. Over in Britain, the Trade Union movement gained in strength and in 1919 the country went through the most severe strike wave they had ever experienced, losing thirty-five million working days in actions taken by the armed forces, miners, transport workers, printers and even the police. The first unions were also forming in Malta with the teachers, the Maltese civil servants and Admiralty clerks leading the way during this incredibly tense period.

On the 17th June of the same year, the youth of Valletta hit the streets causing serious damage to public buildings including the university, the newspaper offices and politician's and mill owner's homes, in an incident that saw the tragic shooting of four rioters by the British army, one of whom was killed. The shock in witnessing the army actually firing on Maltese citizens caused a lull in the uprising that was shattered only the following day when the riot continued with more vigour. Valletta was in near lock down with the marines, being the only troops allowed out of barracks, taking control of the situation until the new Governor, Field-Marshal Viscount Herbert Plumer (gov 1919-1924) arrived. Plumer was a big hitter with his previous job being Commander-in-Chief of the British Army of the Rhine (BAOR), the force formed to occupy defeated Germany after the war. The new Governor arrived in a capital under martial control and when seeing the thousands gathered in Palace Square, he ordered his driver to stop and let him out to walk through the crowds to the palace, where he dismissed most of his guard, immediately introducing an element of calm.

Governor, Field-Marshal Viscount Herbert Plumer (gov 1919-1924)

Plumer worked hard to become the man of the people and made some good reforms along the way, beginning with the introduction of a bread subsidy, he instigated a program of public works creating much needed jobs and organised a £250,000 grant from Britain. More importantly, it was under Plumer that the process began that eventually led to Maltese independence. With the help of Leopold Stennett Amery, the Under Secretary of State for the Colonies, who arrived in Malta in the September of 1919, a two house system, under the Governor, was organised similar to that introduced in India and that would include members elected by the Maltese. The British Parliament agreed to the new Maltese constitution on 20th November and on 3rd December Lord Milner visited Malta to formally announce its introduction, saying;

'We are giving you the engine, it's up to you now to find its engineers'.

Soon the Anglo-Maltese Party, the Constitutional Party, the Democratic Party, the Union Party and the Labour Party were all formed and the process was up and running by 16th May 1921, with Joseph Howarth (pm 1921-1923) being elected as the first Maltese Prime Minister on 26th October 1921.

The road to self rule was interrupted by the growing threat of Italian Nationalism and Fascism that had spread to Malta and by the unhelpful interference of the Vatican, which resulted in the suspension of the island's constitution, initially on 24th June 1930 for a period of two years and again in 1933. At this point it was felt in London that Italian Nationalism was threatening British control over Malta and as a show of strength, the navy moved up to 70 ships over to protect their Crown Colony.

As a matter of public relations the navy opened up many of the ships for visits by the islanders and encouraged young Maltese men to join the service. Attempts to discourage the Italian language were put in position, such as providing scholarships in British universities and introducing the use of Maltese as the language of the law, replacing Italian. On the islands, improvements to infrastructure and utilities could be seen to be taking place in an attempt to renew good feeling towards the British and with the influx of hundreds of sailors, all frequenting the island's bars and shops, things were looking good for a while.

Tensions in respect to the Italian situation were ratcheted up a notch with the so called Abyssinian Crisis of 1935, when Mussolini's forces invaded Abyssinia, (today's Ethiopia), effectively bringing an end to peace in Europe and forming a pact between Fascist Italy and Nazi Germany. From here the political state deteriorated badly as the League of Nations disintegrated and with Hitler's Germany invading Poland on 1st September 1939 the future was sealed. At 11.15 on 3rd September 1939, the British Prime Minister, Neville Chamberlain addressed the nation, via BBC radio, with the ominous message;

'I am speaking to you from the Cabinet Room at 10, Downing Street. This morning the British Ambassador in Berlin handed the German Government a final note stating that unless we heard from them by 11.00 a.m. that they were prepared at once to withdraw their troops from Poland, a state of war would exist between us. I have to tell you that no such undertaking has been received, and that consequently this country is at war with Germany'.

World War II and the 'Second Great Siege'

Whilst the distant drums of war were beating throughout Europe in 1939 no one could be certain of any outcome, or where the potential battle lines where to be drawn. Each country had to prepare for the worst in the best way they could and Malta was no exception. Governor Sir Charles Bonham Carter (gov 1936-1940) began by arranging for committees to be set up in towns and villages, involving leading members of each community, to enable effective communications and organisation if war was to reach the island's shores. Air raid wardens were to be recruited and trained and air raid shelters were to be located in caves and tunnels and in many cases dug out of the soft Globigerina Limestone that was easily worked and would set hard soon after exposure to the air. With permission from the District Committee, private shelters would be dug out to a maximum allowed width of six feet, sometimes connected together with those of neighbours, who would be available to recover each other in the case of collapsed shelters, usually caused by water leakage weakening the rock, or from bomb blasts.

With the outbreak of hostilities on 3rd September defensive arrangements intensified and with Italy's declaration of war on 10th June 1940, the worry of gas attacks must have appeared very real, considering Mussolini's use of mustard gas against the Abyssinians in 1936, ensuring that the distributed gas masks were important assets. To confound the situation it must have appeared that things could not have worked out worse for Malta when France, being an important ally and potential defender, signed an armistice agreement with Germany on 22nd June 1940, effectively removing themselves from the war. The response of the Maltese in the face of the deteriorating situation was one of resolve, as people were being moved en masse from the major centres of population in Valletta, Floriana and the Three Cities, inland to the smaller towns and villages. Any sort of meaningful employment for people became hard to find for the over 80,000 refugees that had been distributed within Malta; with nearly 17,000 in Birkirkara, 13,000 in the old inland capital of Rabat and Mdina and 8,500 in Qormi etc.

The composition of this conflict was now extremely different to that of World War One, where the front line remained well away from Malta; this time the islands were directly vulnerable to the Italian Air Force which boasted 5,400 aircraft in 1940. The Italian Navy was also a strong force in the Mediterranean and with aerial protection from the Air Force and no French interference the islands were left enormously vulnerable. Luckily the British, although now widely stretched, also had naval bases around the Mediterranean, in Gibraltar, Cyprus, Egypt, as well as Malta and crucially, unlike Italy, they had the advantage of radar on the island. Any information gathered would be augmented by that of an underground listening centre in Lascaris, Valletta, that worked closely with Bletchley Park, in England.

The important issue of feeding those on the islands, both the Maltese and military personnel, had to be faced, particularly as even import supplies from Sicily were no longer possible and those by sea could not be relied on. It can not have been an easy strategic decision to concentrate defences on Malta, at the expense of Gozo, which was to be used as a food basket, with the belief that any direct attack on the islands would be concentrated on Malta itself. A Food Control Board was also created to oversee the process of rationing, whilst an Australian, Lieutenant Robert Jackson, took charge of stocking the island so that it could withstand a two year siege. With the benefit of hindsight, Jackson's contribution to the survival of Malta through the proceeding few years could not be overstated. These food stores also provided a safety net in the form of the 'Communal Feeding Service', that those suffering from poverty could apply to for fortnightly hot meal and grocery coupons.

With the health of Bonham Carter failing, it was a new Governor, Sir William Dobbie (gov 1940-1942), that addressed the people on 10th May to ask for the creation of a local defence force. Soon the new 'Malta Volunteer Defence Force' had 3,000 volunteers, all ready to patrol the islands coastlines and countryside keeping a vigilant eye open for parachute landings. A few days later a curfew was introduced, initially from 11pm to 5am, that was bound to assist the MVDF during the hours of darkness. A month later, on the day that Italy joined the war, Dobbie issued a rallying statement to the islands service personnel saying;

'The decision of His Majesty's government to fight until our enemies are defeated will be heard with the greatest satisfaction by all ranks of the Garrison of Malta. It may be that hard times lie ahead of us, but I know that however hard they may be, the courage and determination of all ranks will not falter, and that with God's help we will maintain the security of this fortress. I call on all officers and other ranks humbly to seek God's help, and then in reliance on Him to do their duty unflinchingly.'

Governor, Sir William Dobbie (gov 1940-1942)

Courage and determination would indeed be needed over the proceeding months and years for all those living in the Maltese Islands as the Italian Air Force began to bombard them ruthlessly. In the second half of 1940 alone there were over 200 air raids sending the people running for cover and returning to devastation in wrecked buildings and infrastructure. The carnage could have been much worse though in respect to lives lost and injury, were it not for the island's prepared defences and the Italian's lack of fighter planes to protect the bombers, thus forcing the attacking aircraft to a greater height than they would have preferred for accurate bombing missions.

Britain now moved to protect Malta with the delivery of 12 Hurricane fighter planes on 12th August and the fully equipped and state of the art aircraft carrier HMS Illustrious, together with the battleships Valiant and Warspite and the anti-aircraft cruisers, Coventry and Calcutta. As if this was not enough to lift the spirits of the suffering islanders, the first relief convoy arrived on 1st September to cheers from the crowds gathered above the Grand Harbour. It was now time to return a little of the treatment back in the direction of Italy so on the night of the 11th November, Illustrious sent her Swordfish aircraft, equipped with torpedoes, bombs and flares, to the Taranto naval base, sinking one of Italy's six battleships and causing two others to be beached. This was the first ever total aircraft naval attack and its success made way for a more optimistic mood as Malta moved to the end of a turbulent 1940.

Over in Germany, Hitler and his generals were angry and dismayed that Italy had not taken control of Malta, a major strategic position that would greatly assist in their goal of gaining possession of the Suez Canal and North Africa. They decided to hand the job over to General Geissler and his Tenth Air Corps who moved into position in Sicily, bringing with them a wealth of experience of anti-shipping raids and they meant business. Their main objective was to defeat the allied Mediterranean fleet and this meant the destruction of HMS Illustrious.

Malta & Gozo - A Megalithic Journey

HMS Illustrious and a Swordfish being loaded with a torpedo

So far Malta had received supplies from four convoys and now they were expecting a further one, 'Operation Excess', that on the morning of 10th January 1941 had crossed the Atlantic, passed through the Straits of Gibraltar and reached its rendezvous point off Sicily, from were they were to be escorted into Malta by the Mediterranean fleet. It had reached early afternoon when the radar on board Illustrious picked up two large groups of aircraft approaching from Sicily and it was not long before the first German onslaught began. Forty-three Junkers Ju87 'Stuka' dive-bombers poured their deadly cargo of 1,000 lb bombs onto the decks of the aircraft carrier causing massive damage both above and more seriously below decks, where the fires raged up to 60 degrees C. When Illustrious finally limped into Malta's Grand Harbour at 21.45 she was in a terrible condition, needing extensive repairs. The convoy ships, though, had slipped through whilst Illustrious had received the bombardment, so the island, at least, received its much needed supplies and reinforcements.

Sitting along side Parlatorio Wharf on French Creek in Malta's Grand Harbour, work was to begin immediately on the crippled HMS Illustrious so that she could at least head off to a safer place. In fact General Geissler considered the bombing of the ship as unfinished work and as early as 13th January daily air raids began in what is remembered as 'the Illustrious blitz'. The collateral damage to surrounding buildings and shipping during this extensive bombing campaign was massive, leaving many dead and wounded. Then under the darkness of the night of the 23rd January, HMS Illustrious slid stealthily out of Grand Harbour, safely reaching Alexandria three days later, from where it sailed to Norfolk, Virginia in the independent USA, for a complete renovation.

*HMS Illustrious under attack in the Grand Harbour
(To the right of the large crane)*

It might have appeared in Malta that the most difficult times were over when the level of air attacks reduced and the sirens were heard less often over the islands, whilst a large part of the German Tenth Air Corps moved away to support General Rommel in north Africa. But it was this very area of conflict that was soon to put the relative calm under threat again as Rommel reported back to Hitler that the taking of the strategically positioned Malta was essential to his efforts. In Malta, Governor Dobbie introduced conscription in the February, to help prepare for the worst and to provide much needed employment for many, and in the mean time the islanders took a deep breath. When the bombing came again it was from the combined German and Italian air forces, mainly aimed at the Grand Harbour and the airfields and it was regular, daily and deadly. In April, when the Catholic Maltese were concentrating on the Easter festival, the old capital of Mdina was bombed even though it was a purely inland residential area with no military significance. At the end of the same month heavy day and night time bombing concentrated on Valletta itself, damaging St John's Co-Cathedral and demolishing many other buildings.

In the face of this constant bombardment Dobbie wanted to strike back and with the arrival of a fleet of submarines to be based at Malta, he ordered that the enemy supply lines to North Africa, via Tripoli, be attacked, even whilst the German and Italian forces where attempting to disrupt the allied supplies as they crossed the Mediterranean eastward. By May a large quantity of Hurricane MKIIA aeroplanes had been delivered to Malta to aid in defence as well as offensive operations and, together with Wellington Bombers, they took part in hundreds of sorties over Italy throughout the summer months. By the end of 1941 Italy had abandoned the supply route north across the Mediterranean at around the time that Malta was welcoming convoy GM2 that was to offload a massive 85,000 tons of supplies and some 2,600 relief troops. Things appeared to be going well but this feeling was not to last very long as Germany began to put the squeeze on Malta.

As 1942 dawned the Mediterranean fleet was taking severe damage having not recovered from losses gained at the German invasion of Crete the previous May and they were now statistically no match for the Italian Navy.

Malta & Gozo - A Megalithic Journey

Hurricane MKIIA Fighter and Wellington MK II Bomber

Without adequate protection vessels, gaining any sort of supplies became extremely difficult, even a delivery of potatoes ready for planting was sunk putting the yearly harvest at risk. On top of this the German 'Luftwaffe' increased its bombing campaign massively and with it the casualty rate soared, whilst many Allied aircraft were destroyed where they stood.

Spitfires in Tunisia before moving to Malta in March 1942

In February Squadron Leader Stan Taylor arrived in Malta to take over the 249 Squadron and he immediately called out for an urgent delivery of Spitfire fighter planes and on 7th March fifteen of these were flown in from the aircraft carrier, HMS Eagle off Algiers. On the 21st March a further sixteen spitfires were flown from the two aircraft carriers the Angus and the Eagle, as part of a convoy through Gibraltar, whilst a second consecutive convoy left Alexandria also bound for Malta. Both convoys came under massive fire from both ships and the air and only three merchant ships got to the harbour and survived long enough to unload some of their cargo, before they sank. Of the 26,000 tons of supplies convoyed to Malta in the first quarter of 1942, only 5,000 got through.

The level of Luftwaffe air attacks on Malta continued at an enormous pace with over 15,500 buildings destroyed in the beginning of April causing over 1,100 deaths and 2,500 injuries. The spitfire attacks were also causing great damage to enemy aircraft but it seemed to make little to no difference as the air raids continued relentlessly. As Easter came around again the island was receiving an average of a dozen air raids every day with 6,000 sorties recorded in April alone, whilst ammunition for the defensive guns was running out fast. During one of the Easter attacks, on the 9th April, a famous episode occurred that is well remembered today, when a 2,000 lb bomb fell through the dome roof of the Mosta church, landing in the centre of the circular building without exploding and miraculously there were no injuries.

It was in the same month and in the midst of such terrible devastating attacks that on 15th April 1942, King George VI awarded the George Cross to the people of Malta. Governor Dobbie received the award which read;

'To honour her brave people I award the George Cross to the Island Fortress of Malta to bear witness to a heroism and devotion that will long be famous in history.', (signed) George R.I.

Mosta Church and the inside of the Dome

To which he replied with the words;

'By God's help Malta will not weaken but will endure until victory is won.'

It was not until 13th September that a public ceremony on Palace Square, Valletta took place, where Governor John Vereker, the Viscount Gort (gov 1942-1944) presented the award to Sir George Borg, the Chief Justice of Malta, on behalf of the people of the island.

Bomb devastation at Kingsway, Valletta's main thoroughfare (1st May 1942)

By the beginning of summer food supplies were getting extremely low and troops, being on half rations, were being ordered to rest when not working in order to preserve strength. Movement around the island was also restricted due to fuel shortages with very few buses in operation and those that did run would only skirt the smaller towns and villages, leaving passengers with miles still to walk.

Plaque on the Presidential Palace

The Maltese George Cross and the award ceremony on 13th September 1942

It was beginning to seem that if supplies where not forthcoming, Malta would be forced to give way to German invasion, a state of affairs that must have appeared more than evident to new Governor, Lord Gort, on his arrival on 7th May. His first action to take control of the situation was to place the whole island on siege rations and work out a 'target date', whereby all food, fuel, ammunition and other resources would run out. The target date turned out to be only eight weeks off, a relatively short time for a successful convey to make its way through heavy bombardment, to arrive at Malta.

The supply attempt was to be in the form of two convoys approaching from different directions to provide the maximum chance of at least one getting through. Operation Harpoon left the UK on 5th June and then Gibraltar on 11th June at the same time as Operation Vigorous was leaving Alexandria which although it was well defended, ran into serious trouble and had to return to port. Operation Harpoon, on the other hand made its way though minefields under heavy sea, air and submarine torpedo attack, and whilst losing several supporting vessels, two supply ships arrived in the Grand Harbour, together with the nippy mine-layer HMS Welshman in support, on 15th June under a heavy smoke screen. 15,000 tons of supplies were hastily offloaded into the empty warehouses but it wasn't going to touch the sides; Malta needed much more if it was going to survive.

Plans for the surrender of the Maltese Islands were quietly being prepared in London as the Target Date, now in August, was quickly approaching. This would be a terrible loss in many ways for the Maltese people and for the British, both strategically and for morale and it could heavily influence the outcome of the war. It was felt that a final all-out effort should be attempted and this was to be the now famous convoy 'Operation Pedestal', better known to the Maltese as the 'Santa Marija Convoy' after the feast of the Assumption of the Virgin Mary, held on 15th August and in 1942 this was an even more important date as by then the future of Malta would be known.

Shot of Operation Pedestal from HMS Victorious, with HMS Indomitable and the soon to be lost HMS Eagle to the rear

The Operation Pedestal convoy was going to be huge due mainly to the amount of protection vessels which would crucially include the naval air coverage that had been missing on recent relief attempts. Heavy loss of ships was thought inevitable so no less than fourteen merchant vessels set off, loaded with supplies, more ships than Malta could have coped with. The convoy was to be protected by 'Force Z', possibly to indicate the final attempt, and it was commanded by Vice Admiral Syfret with the battleships HMS Nelson and Rodney, four aircraft carriers, seven cruisers and 32 destroyers. Additionally they would be supported by two fuel tankers, three small Corvette warships, a tug and eight submarines when they got nearer to their destination.

Operation Pedestal, under heavy air attack on 11th August 1942, HMS Rodney left, HMS Manchester right

The convoy left the UK over the night of 2nd/3rd August, arriving at the Straits of Gibraltar early on 10th August where they refuelled for the difficult passage through the Mediterranean. Each Merchant captain had been given a sealed envelope to be opened at 8am on this day from the First Sea Lord wishing them 'God Speed' and they were going to need it. As the convoy continued on its easterly journey a dummy fleet was heading westward from along the North African coast to confuse the enemy and draw fire for a short while before returning to port. On the 11th August the aged HMS Eagle was torpedoed and eventually sunk and HMS Furious headed back to Gibraltar after successfully completing its mission of sending off 37 Spitfires to Malta, to be of great help later. The Luftwaffe attacked a couple of times during the day and again at noon. They were then joined by the Italians for a joint attack of 100 aircraft, sinking one merchant vessel and putting HMS Indomitable out of action, followed later by another onslaught that sank HMS Cairo, two more Merchant ships and damaging four other vessels, including the Ohio that was later to be helped into Grand Harbour. By the end of the day another six ships were sunk including HMS Manchester, but the remaining convoy continued steadily on its way, gradually getting nearer to its destination. The following day, the 12th August, saw more air attack and HMS Ohio, already damaged, was blazing to the point that the captain ordered the crew to abandon ship. Amazingly Ohio remained afloat for so long that the crew climbed back on board. Force Z, having escorted the convoy within the last 36 hours of arriving at Malta, handed it over to Force X to lead it through the dangerous Sicilian Channel encouraged that they were now within Spitfire range.

On 13th August more ships were being lost and seriously damaged but finally four merchant ships arrived in the Grand Harbour and Ohio was towed and assisted in by the destroyer Penn and two minesweepers the Rye and the Ledbury, arriving on 15th August with the fuel that was to be so critical to survival and ongoing offence. Malta had just thirteen days of supplies left before the success of Operation Pedestal refilled the island's warehouses and fuel tanks, the price had been terrible but the outcome meant that Malta would remain in British hands and although it was not the end of the siege, it indicated easier times to come.

HMS Ohio being escorted into Grand Harbour

The war in North Africa became an important focus with the Suez Canal being the prize sought by the rival generals Montgomery and Rommel and Malta's position in the centre of the Mediterranean was again of strategic importance. To this end a new runway was constructed at Qrendi, known as 'Safi' and the number of aircraft based on the island was increased in order to maintain air support and a constant bombing campaign on Sicilian airfields clearing the way for shipping. A further indication of better times was the arrival in Malta of Operation Stoneage on 23rd November 1942, a relief convoy of four merchant ships from Alexandria, the first one to make the journey without being attacked since 1940. The final air raids over Malta took place on 26th February 1943 indicating that the siege had ended and then in May 1943 in an outcome that was to prove a turning point in the war the German Afrika Korps surrendered to the Allied forces after defeat at the battle of El Alamein.

American forces landing on Sicily during Operation Husky

It was just the following month that Malta received a royal visit, when on the 20th June HMS Aurora sailed into Grand Harbour with King George VI standing on deck wearing the uniform of the Admiral of the Fleet. The combined sound of church bells from Valletta and each of the Three Cities that surrounded the harbour, welcomed the King and the masses covered every inch of the bastions to cheer the monarch's arrival. Whether it was the King's first hand experience of the devastation of Malta's infrastructure or not, the British Parliament soon organised a payment of £30,000,000 to help rebuild the island. The respite from the ending of the bombing and the constant air-raid sirens followed by the royal visit must have provided a welcome relief for the tired and worn out people of Malta, who although in a mood to celebrate, were still aware of unfinished business; there remained a war to be won.

The military build-up on Malta began anew with the number of fighter and bomber aircraft reaching a massive 600 & Grand Harbour becoming packed with British navy vessels, this time to including numerous landing craft. The planned objective, Operation Husky, began on 9th July 1943 when allied forces successfully invaded Sicily before continuing on to the Italian mainland on 3rd September. Back in Malta the feast day of Our Lady of Victories was taking place in Senglea, one of the Three Cities, where the streets were packed with Maltese from around the island, celebrating the defeat of the Ottoman Turks in 1565. The parish priest began his address to the gathered masses with the words;

'My brethren, rejoice, I have just had the news that Italy has surrendered'. (Wragg, David, *Malta, The Last Great Siege 1940-1943.* p 217).

It was the 8th September 1943, a date that the people of Malta will never forget. Within a few days the confiscated Italian fleet of up to 65 ships sat outside Grand Harbour and Admiral Sir Andrew Cunningham, sent the message to the Admiralty;

'Pleased to inform their Lordships that the Italian battle fleet now lies at anchor under the guns of the fortress of Malta'. (Wragg, David, Malta, The Last Great Siege 1940-1943. pg 217).

Even though World War Two was to continue for another two years, it was now up to others to bring this blemish on our history to a close, for Malta had played her part and it was now time to rebuild and reflect. The Maltese people had been through a baptism of fire, they had seen their beloved island torn to shreds and lived through a devastating siege. Although returning to the more simple pre-war life under the ruler ship of a foreign power must have seemed appealing to many, is that possible after such an initiation?

Towards Independence

Post war Malta brought with it a tangible void; the bombing had ceased and many of the British service personnel were heading home, the airfields were now quiet and the huge contingency of ships in the Grand Harbour reduced considerably. For many years the Maltese economy had relied significantly on the British military presence for its strength and success, through employment in the shipyards and factories, and with the logistical industry that surrounded them, not to mention the hundreds of hungry and thirsty soldiers, sailors and airmen whose appetites would be catered for in the cities' bars and cafes. Now at a time when the future of all this was not certain, there was talk of a greater measure of self-rule and even independence.

With the British administration legalising and seemingly encouraging the Maltese Trade Union movement in 1945, strikes began as jobs disappeared and it became clear that a new plan of some sort was needed to paint a picture of Malta's future. Self-government was the first step with an election in September 1947 resulting in the Maltese Labour Party, backed by the newly invigorated trade unions, taking power with 24 seats and with the Nationalists taking only 7. The new Labour Government was going to have to think outside of the box as it could not just rely on British defence spending for its economic success; it would have to utilize the skills sets it had developed through the war years and find avenues for diversification.

The question as to Malta's ongoing relationship with Britain was addressed at joint discussion sessions that took place in London and Valletta whereby strategies put forward by the political parties, ranging from complete independence, through the total integration of Malta into the British state, to direct colonial rule, were considered. An outcome appeared to have been reached in 1955 when a report from London announced that in theory Malta could have direct representation at Westminster with political integration. This fundamental and original decision could have merged the two countries together permanently, but it reckoned without the intervention of the Catholic Church who had strong objections to Malta integrating into a Protestant country. Nevertheless the matter was put to a referendum which drew such a small turnout that, whether or not this was due to the churches intervention, the plan had to be dropped.

As if the strategic value of Malta's position in the Mediterranean had to be reminded to all concerned, Egyptian President Colonel Nasser, in a surprise move on 26th July 1956, nationalized the Suez Canal Company, until then owned by a British-French consortium. The military build up in Malta was evocative of the invasion of Sicily, with 100 ships prepared for the air and sea attack of Egypt that took place later in the year after Israel and Russia became involved in the issue, with the affair ending in a ceasefire on 7th November when American President Dwight Eisenhower refused support.

British and Maltese infighting led to the island's constitution being removed in 1959, in an action that perhaps deliberately produced anger amongst the islanders and increased calls for independence. The British Government's response was to produce a five year plan for the development of Malta's economy, mainly in the areas of tourism, agriculture and new industry, at a cost of £32 million of which Britain was to finance around two thirds. The successful introduction of this plan would put Malta in a much more favourable position for independence, whilst the constant cutting of the British military budget encouraged the reduction of Malta's dependence on it. Further to this a constitutional committee was set up in 1960, by Sir Hilary Blood, that produced a report on movements towards self-government and a 'State of Malta'.

Nevertheless the situation of Britain's relationship with Malta was to be decided by general election in 1962 when the Nationalists won 25 seats and Labour 16, where both parties had included independence in their election mandates. Dr Borg Olivier, the leader of the Nationalists, now as Prime Minister of Malta, made an official request that Malta was to be given independence in 1964, which was granted by the British Government. The ceremonies were carried out on 20th September with pomp and ceremony at Floriana Parade Ground, where the Constitutional Instruments of

Independence were presented to Dr Borg Olivier by Prince Philip, making Malta an independent state. The Maltese flag was hoisted at midnight, replacing the Union Jack to huge cheering, and the party continued into the night.

All ties were not broken though as Malta remained part of the British Commonwealth with the reigning monarch as head of state, and to ease the changeover for both sides, a defence agreement was entered into whereby a military presence would remain on the island until 1974. With this continued involvement between the two states, the Governor, Sir Maurice Doorman (gov 1962-1971) was to be the last Briton to hold the post.

The issue of payment to Malta for the usage of the island as a military base now became an issue with Borg Olivier taking a hard stance, so much so that after much negotiation and brinkmanship, Britain began the process of evacuation in 1972. Then an unexpected last minute agreement was signed on 26th March by the Prime Ministers, Dom Mintoff and Lord Carrington, that British forces were to remain in Malta until 31st March 1979, at a rent of £14 million per annum, payable by Britain and NATO, with additional aid payments.

Malta's aim was now for total independence and the next step took place on 13th December 1974, when it became a republic, within the Commonwealth but removing the British monarch as the head of state, with the General Governor taking over the role as President. Just as planned, Malta reached it's goal, when on 31st March 1979 thousands gathered to watch the last British armed forces leave the island after 181 years.

Chapter 6

Malta Today
(From 1964)

If there was to be any apprehension leading up to Maltese independence in 1964 and its republican status in 1974, it was not to last long and over the intervening years the islands have developed an 'advanced economy', under the classification of the International Monetary Fund. At the turn of the 19th Century, Malta's exports mainly included cotton and tobacco, supported by domestic farming, and when Britain took over control of the island it's extensive military budget resulted in the growth of the shipyards. The Maltese economy developed an unbalanced reliance on naval and shipping related industries, a situation that caused anxiety as the island's leaders strived towards much needed diversification. Today tourism has filled some of the void created by the loss of a military industry, with 1.7 million visitors in 2014, the majority of which arrive from the United Kingdom, more then tripling the resident population of around 450,000 on Malta and 31,000 on Gozo. Nearly 500,000 of the holiday visitor numbers derive from cruise ships calling for single days at a time and thus not using the island's hotels and catering outlets.

The islands position at a narrow point in the Mediterranean and in the shipping lanes puts it in an ideal location for its essential foreign trade that includes exports of electronics and pharmaceuticals, and the development of banking and financial services have become an important source of income. The fact that Malta can only produce 20% of its food usage also emphasises the importance of its foreign trade positioning. It could be said though, that the Maltese economy has been a great success over the last ten years with a Gross Domestic Product of around 7.5 million Euros in 2013 (18.75 Eu. per head).

It is generally considered that the relatively small size of the domestic Maltese market made the joining of the European Union on 1st May 2004 a forgone conclusion due to the beneficial effects of the extended market. In 2008 the process of Malta's European integration became complete with the joining of the currency 'Eurozone', giving up the island's Lira or Pound that it had used since leaving the British Pound in 1972, and taking up the Euro.

The Maltese Government's keenness to encourage external investment can be demonstrated in its financing of the film industry that began in 1925 with the filming of the 'Sons of the Sea' and the popular island tourist attraction 'Popeye Village', is a film set from 1980. The film industry has provided a substantial income of approx 25 million Euros in the decade to 2011, producing and hosting around 100 feature films in its time, including 'Gladiator', 'Troy', 'Munich' and 'The Count of Monte Cristo'.

The Maltese Islands can be seen today as an economically successful independent state, at peace with itself and the rest of the world. It's excellent year-round climate make it attractive to holiday makers and tourists from around Europe and the rest of the world. The islands have a unique history, as portrayed above, with some of the most fascinating ancient and historical sites, that are unequalled anywhere.

Part 2

Ancient and Historical Sites of Malta and Gozo

Chapter 7

Valletta and Eastern Malta

Busy Republic Street, Valetta

Valletta, the capital of Malta, is a vibrant modern city covering the entire peninsula of Mount Sceberras that points to the northeast out over the Mediterranean from eastern Malta, by far the most densely populated area of the island. The city began life with the laying of the foundation stone in 1566 when the then Grand Master of the Knights of St John, Jean

Parisot de Valette, decide to move the administrative centre of the Order from Birgu (Vittoriosa), in the Three Cities area.

Aligned with fashionable shops, Valletta's main thoroughfare is Republic Street stretching from the City Gates, for one kilometre along the spine of Mount Sceberras down to Fort St Elmo. Streets fall off to each side forming a grid-square design of 0.8 Km2 (0.3 sq miles), right down to the waters edge of the Grand Harbour to the south and Marsamxett Harbour to the north. The fine buildings of the busy commercial and financial areas, ranging from the 16th century Baroque to the Modern period, lie in close proximity to residential housing with their long lines of distinctive colourful balconies.

The ramparts of this magnificent city have witnessed numerous battles and repelled many invaders, not the least during World War Two and the 'Fort St Elmo, National War Museum' is a fitting memorial to these more difficult times. Today though the fortifications welcome tourists from throughout the World to explore its many attractions that include many fine religious buildings and palaces, the Upper and Lower Barakka gardens and the Auberges or old headquarters of the Knights of St John. The audiovisual show, 'The Malta Experience', situated on the bastions of Fort St Elmo and depicting 7,000 years of the island's history, is a great place to begin any visit of the islands.

The 'built-up' feeling of this eastern section of the island will become evident when visiting the Tarxien Temples and the Hypogeum Hal Saflieni, both quite near to each other in the town of Paola. Whilst the tourist areas of Sliema and St Julian's, to the north of Valetta are good for accommodation and for evenings out in the many restaurants and bars, time is also well spent by visiting Birgu (Vittoriosa), in the Three Cities. This small town on the edge of the sea was inhabited from at least as far ago as the Roman Period and it is here that the Knights of St John decided to settle when they landed on Malta in 1530, under the protection of the Medieval Castrum Maris, or Sea Castle, which became the imposing Fort St Angelo that still stands today. Just along from the Castle, past the old warehouses of the knights and usually a display of large luxury power yachts, is the 'Malta Maritime Museum' and above on Triq Il-Palazz Ta' L-Isqof, the 'Inquisitor's Palace'.

The National Museum of Archaeology Valletta

The National Museum of Archaeology

The 'National Museum of Archaeology' is easily located in a fine baroque building on Valletta's Republic Street. Dating from 1571, it used to be the Auberge, or headquarters, of the Provence Language of the Knights of St John. The museum provides essential information on the island's pre-history and including a visit here to any tour of Malta is highly recommended and well worth the entry fee.

Interesting features greet you as soon as you enter the lobby area where the ceiling is opulently painted, probably by Nocolò Nasoni (1691-1769), with a central design depicting a figure in the clouds holding a sword and shield of the Knights. You then pass between the two iconic giant spiral carvings recovered from the Tarxien Temples before going though the barriers to enter the main display area. Here the exhibits are separated into six rooms.

Stone with the giant spiral carvings

The journey through Malta's pre-history begins in Room One where the visitor is taken back to the very early Neolithic Age by providing examples of pottery from the Ghar Dalam Period (5200-4500 BC) and in chronological order through Grey

Skorba (4500-4400 BC), Red Skorba (4400-4100 BC) and down to Zebbug (4100-3700 BC). Being able to view the differences and variations between the various pottery periods brings to life these early time periods that can appear arbitrary when only seen in photographs. Also in this area are various sewing and inscribing implements and ornaments including very early human figurines, mainly produced from Red Skorba clay. The extremely important question of human burial is covered by a cross-cut display of a rock-cut tomb, showing a positioned skeleton and possibly a suggestion as to where the shape of the future apse came from, although this is an extremely subjective suggestion.

In Room Two you are moved forward in time into the Temple Period (from 4100 BC), firstly with a section covering the Ħal Saflieni Hypogeum which includes an interesting and detailed model of the site. Further models of the Ġgantija, Mnajdra and Ħaġer Qim temples show the development and growth of design over the period with pictorial comment boards explaining this progression. Next to these are two rather randomly positioned stone altars from the Tarxien Temple of spindle or hourglass design. Various other implements and tools of bone, flint, chert and obsidian are displayed in one area with small design models and shards, probably from the trestle table at the temple planning phase, in another. Of these template models the one in Showcase 9 is of particular interest, uncovered at the Ta' Ħaġrat Temple, it is complete with a roof thus putting it right at the centre of the debate as to the overall design of roofing on all of the temples.

There is an animal theme to the collection of large blocks from the Tarxien Temple, unusually depicting rows of bulls, sheep, pigs and rams, although part of this set are copies with the originals still in situ. If there is a meaning to the animal feature it has been lost in time as has the reason for the highly decorative floral designs on the four sided pedestal with concave top that is to be found nearby, again from Tarxien.

Another feature of great interest and much discussion is the collection of large stone balls that have been recovered from the temples and are said by some to have been used as bearings to roll the stone orthostatic stones into place, but the fact that the balls were also found at the Hypogeum, where there are no such megaliths as the walls are all carved out of the rock, appears to dispel this argument. What other possible uses these spherical artefacts could have had for our ancient ancestors we are free to debate.

The theme in Room Three is human statuary and figurines and none can be more significant and universally recognizable than the so called 'fat lady', from Tarxien that would have stood up to 3m tall. The rounded 'Goddess' form of this iconic figure is possibly the derivation of the shape of the temple apses, although it has to be remembered that this would only fit the plan perfectly in the case of a four apse temple and the figure could be said to be asexual. The other figure, this time from Tas-Silġ, appears to be of the same image although the top portion has been badly worn away. The same basic corpulent design can be seen in the collection of sitting figurines recovered from the Ħaġer Qim temples, although these range from 50-75cm and have only holes where heads could probably be added and changed as required. Whatever the reason this may have been done, only a few heads have been found and displayed. The other small figures displayed around the room vary greatly in design and type indicating that the activities associated with the temples were complex and multifunctional. Of particular interest are the nine stones with heads and straight bodies found at the Xagħra Stone Circle on Gozo, that might have been funerary gifts and also the only double depiction of the corpulent design with both figures sitting together.

In Room Four is a collection of bizarre and unusual artefacts such as a possible sunstone and a wonderful stone divided into sections, one containing the Moon and the others full of stars. Two pieces, a pebble and a crafted cylinder, show an intriguing but unexplained design with three lines and a fourth running horizontal along one edge. The remainder of this room displays pottery and jewellery from the period including a fine collection of pendants fashioned from shells, stone and faience.

Room Five contains one of the museum's premier artefacts; the 'Sleeping Lady', from the Ħal Saflieni Hypogeum. This clay statue of the corpulent type is intricately detailed but again it's meaning, if any, has been obscured by time. The only other items displayed in this room are two figures also from the Hypogeum but not so well preserved, one is of a sleeping lady lying face down whilst the other could be similar but can not be well defined.

Room Six is the home for some huge blocks of stone removed mainly from the Tarxien Temples to protect the spiral carving and pitting that adorn them whilst replica replacements have been placed in the appropriate positions in the temples.

It is now time to head up the wide staircase to the Grand Salon, a large and wonderfully elegant room on the first floor, with extravagantly painted walls and carved beam ceilings.

This space, that used to be an important meeting place for the Knights, is now the home to extensive and unmissable displays covering the Islands Bronze Age and Phoenician/Punic period.

St John's Co-Cathedral Valletta

Elaborately decorated nave of St John's Co-Cathedral

There is quite a selection of churches in Valletta but St John's Co-Cathedral has earned its place here because of its historical connection with the Knights of St John to whom this was their convent church for over 200 years. What the early knights would have thought of the extremely elaborate decoration that covers the entire interior of the building can only be guessed at but a visit does shine a light on the character of this order that continually changed with the times in order to survive. Time can be spent at the chapels to the various langues of the order that are spread throughout the interior of the building and to explore the fine details of the flamboyant décor that is far too complex to be described here. On arrival an audio guide is provided after the payment of an entrance fee and the cathedral is extremely easy to locate being right in the middle of Valletta and half way down the central thoroughfare of Republic Street.

The Knights of St John were awarded the island of Malta in 1530 by Emperor Charles V of Spain and they settled in Birgu in what is now part of the Three Cities. In 1565 their principle enemy the Ottomans laid siege to Malta and although the Knights eventually fought off their foe they had taken extensive damage. In 1566 Grand Mater Jean de Valette founded the city that was to be named after him and that would provide the protection they would require. Part of this vast project would be this church that was to be central to the city and the order and work began under the control of the Maltese architect Gerolamo Cassar in 1572. The church only took five years to complete and it was constructed out of the local globigerina limestone to produce a rather plain exterior in adherence to the knight's three monastic vows of chastity, obedience and poverty. It was from the balcony over the main entrance, between the two rather stern looking bell towers that successive Grand Masters would address the people gathered on St John's Square.

The church was dedicated to St John the Baptist, the patron saint of the Order and was founded by Grand Master Jean l'Evesque da la Cassiere, who created chapels for each langue. Originally the walls of the church and its chapels would have been plain and in fitting with the Orders vows but permission was granted to decorate the building under Grand Master Alof de Wignacourt (GM 1601-1622). It was in the 17th Century that the flamboyant Baroque style was in full bloom and decorative work was carried out in this fashion that was to totally transform the church into the fantastically elaborate finish that can be seen today.

The famous Italian painter Mattia Preti (Il Calabrese), joined the order of St John as a knight of obedience in 1642 and was given the commission of the painting of the church vault followed by works in some of the langue chapels. The contrast to the original severe interior and the present exterior of the building with the ostentatious 'Venetian Opulence' style of Preti's work, amongst others, must have been immense and maybe it is this that most reflects the changing times of the Order of St John, that became the Knights of Malta.

The Presidential Palace Valletta

The Presidential Palace, Valletta

The most striking building on Valletta's main thoroughfare of Republic Street is the fine Baroque style Presidential Palace, situated halfway down and facing onto Palace Square and the Main Guard Building. The construction of the new city of Valletta was initiated by Grand Master Jean de Valette in 1566, the year following the end of the Great Siege, where the Knights of St John successfully repelled Ottoman invaders. The palace was then designed and built by the Maltese architect Girolamo Cassar in the early 1570s under the instruction of Grand Master Pierre de Monte and completed under the supervision of Jean l'Evesque de la Cassière. This impressive mansion was constructed to incorporate two existing buildings; the Italian Auberge and the house of Eustachio del Monto, a relative of Jean Valetta. The Palace was to house the Grand Masters of the Knights of St John until it passed to the French in 1798 for just a few months, before acting as the British Governor's Palace until the island's Independence in 1964 and is now the Maltese Presidential Palace. The palace was also the seat of Malta's first constitutional parliament from 1921 until the completion of a new Parliamentary Building in 2015. The basic building has been altered and added to numerous times over the years and has always been a storehouse of artworks and historic artefacts.

The front elevation of the palace, whilst undoubtedly having a grand if somewhat plain appearance, is somewhat unsymmetrical due to the effects of having to include the original buildings. The windows in the right hand section of the building, being part of the Eustachio house with smaller rooms, are closer together than those on the left and the position of the entrance after the fifth window from right has been somewhat forced as it marks the end of the same house. This doorway leads though to Prince Alfred's Courtyard complete with stone lions, a wonderful clock from 1745 depicting Moorish slaves striking gongs and a doorway through to the Great Hall.

There are two more entrances to the Palace, one on the western elevation opening onto Republic Square and the other on the left hand part of the front elevation and it is this that leads through to one of two large courtyards around which the palace was formed. This one is the Neptune Courtyard named after the 17th Century bronze statue of the Roman God of the sea that is located there surrounded by archways on the lower level. As is typical for buildings of the period, the lower level would be used for servant's quarters, stables and storage etc, whilst the main business would take place on an upper level and here visitors can take a spiral staircase to the first floor State Rooms when parliament is not sitting and after purchasing a ticket from Heritage Malta.

The splendour of the State Rooms meets you as you land on the long Piano Noble Corridor with its escutcheon style painted ceiling from the 18th century by Nicolau Nasoni. Continuing you pass more splendid artwork, suits of armour, coats of arms and portraits of various Grand Masters of the Knights and entrances to the various rooms of interest.

To the left the Council Chamber is hung with a fine and probably priceless collection of tapestries called the, 'Les Teintures des Indes'. These were commissioned by Grand Master Ramón de Perellos and woven in the Gobelins factory in Paris. They depict tropical scenes and an assortment of exotic animals and plants. Next along, the Dining Room is a veritable portrait gallery that survived the bombing damage of World War II. These are of the island's historic Heads of State including those of the British monarchs together with works that run up to date.

This is followed by the Throne Room which used to be known as the Supreme Council Hall. This would have originally been the meeting place for the Council as well as to entertain Heads of State and VIPs from around the World and other important state occasions. Then, when on the 28th April 1818 the British Administration created the chivalric 'Order of St Michael and St George', they renamed the hall after it whilst having it redecorated in neo-classical style, designed by Lieutenant-Colonel George Whitmore, all of which was removed again in the early 20th century. This room is again wonderfully decorated from its coffered ceilings with arches that stretch from wall to wall with below this, around the upper potion of the wall, are fantastic friezes of the Great Siege of Malta of 1565, painted by Matteo Perez d'Aleccio and a reason on their own to visit the palace. The rather modest throne itself sits at the far end of the Hall surrounded by a Masonic-like pillared backdrop incorporating the arms of the Republic of Malta. Opposite this is the Minstrel's Gallery, said to be part of the Great Carrack of Rhodes, the ship that led the Order when it left Rhodes. This is painted with scenes from the book of Genesis and the coat-of-arms of Grandmaster Jean de Valette. This relic is said to have been in the Grand Master's private chapel until moved here during the time of the British Administration.

A door from the Throne Room leads to the Hall of the Ambassadors, adorned with furniture from the Louis XV period, it is also known as the Red Room due to the colour of its wall coverings. This is where the Grand Master of the time would meet guests and it is now often used for small ceremonial occasions such as the receiving of awards. There are portraits of Grand Masters here and artworks depicting occasions in the Order's history. A further door leads to the Pages' Waiting room and then though to the Grand Master's private rooms which are not on view to visitors.

Returning to the ground floor of the courtyard, the Palace Armoury holds what is one of the best collections of authentic weapons in the World, from the times of the Knights of St John. Tragically during the short period of French occupation of Malta from 1798, much of this irreplaceable collection was broken up through pilfering but despite this a large enough compilation of suits of armour, swords, shields etc, from throughout Europe remain to produce a display with a real wow factor. Some of the pieces can be individualized for example the armour of Grand Masters Jean de Vallete and Alof de Wignacourt and there is even a section for captured Turkish armour and weaponry including the sword of the Greek Ottoman Dragut.

The Ħal Saflieni Hypogeum

The Ħal Saflieni Hypogeum

Human burial on the Maltese islands has always been an issue that involves hard work, mainly because the soil covering is quite thin and so it has often been considered necessary to dig into the limestone to create what are known as rock-cut tombs. The St Paul's and St Agatha's Catacombs, in Rabat, are well known rock-cut burials from the Roman and early Christian periods and similar, less sophisticated burials from the Zebbug Period (4100 BC), at the beginning of the Temple Period, can be seen at Xemxija. It is probable that the island's population grew significantly as the Temple Period progressed and the great stone monuments began to be built in the Ggantija Period (3600 BC). This would have led to a much increased need for burials and it appears that the answer to this was found in combining many graves together on a community rather than a family basis. It would appear from the complex nature of the Hypogeum and in the Rabat tombs, that burial rites and practices also developed significantly and that ancestor memory, if not reverence, was considered important. How many such burials lie silently beneath the now built up areas of Malta, we will probably never find out but we do know that the Hal Saflieni Hypogeum had begun its role by 4000 BC.

This amazing monument might never have been brought to light as it was discovered in 1902 at a time when the increase in available employment in the British military naval yards was attracting many workers to the area resulting in much housing development over the existing field systems. By the time the discovery of the Hypogeum came to the knowledge of the authorities, the site was already being built over and supporting arches and foundation were in place to protect the new homes above, parts of which can still be seen today. The original excavations were carried out by Manwel Magri, but unfortunately his report was lost after his death during missionary work in Tunisia, but the middle and lower areas he had uncovered were opened to the public in January 1908. It was left to Themistocles Zammit to complete Magri's work from 1906 and reports were again made in 1952 as part of a general survey of the Maltese sites. Further excavations were carried out in 1990/93.

Today the amount of visitors to the Hypogeum are extremely limited for conservation purposes and booking early is highly recommended. Passing through the narrow streets of Paola, any expectations of an ostentatious frontage to this celebrated archaeological site are immediately depleted by the small entrance and the narrow benches of the waiting area. When your time comes, you make your way past the information boards to join your group in an audio visual show before being led on a visit controlled by lights that fade in and out as the recorded commentary guides you around the site on a fenced walk way. The limits on access are, of course, in position to protect from wear as are the climate control devices situated around the site.

Excavations indicated that a surface shrine would have marked the location of the Hypogeum, with a passageway leading down from it and on entering the site various stones, probably from this structure, can be made out including one complete trilithon. In the main area of the upper level, that lies a couple of metres below the outside streets, are three deep rock cut tombs with trilithon entrances dating from the Zebbug, at the beginning of the Temple Period. Continuing into this most early part of the monument you see carved burial chambers off to the sides with a deep water cistern to the rear that was probably used to supply water for workers and for ceremonies. The Upper Level appears to have been a typical, if adapted, rock-cut tomb site like that at Xemxija (see below). The need for further burial space led the digging downward where a second level, known as the Middle Level, was carved out and it is this incredible space that has earned the Hypogeum its status as a World class pre-historical site.

In the area between these two levels are a number of side chambers, one of which contains the remains of a human burial left, probably as an exhibit, from Zammit's excavation. The Main Chamber is visible here with its elaborately carved copies of the above ground temple facades and other symmetrical designs and chamber openings, some false but others opening up to new areas. This was one of the rooms that had been painted with red ochre and the remains of various spiral and honeycomb designs can be found throughout this level. Many burial goods were recovered during excavation including; beads, amulets, axe heads and small carved animals and birds and of course the most treasured find of all, the Sleeping Lady, that can now be found in the National Museum of Archaeology.

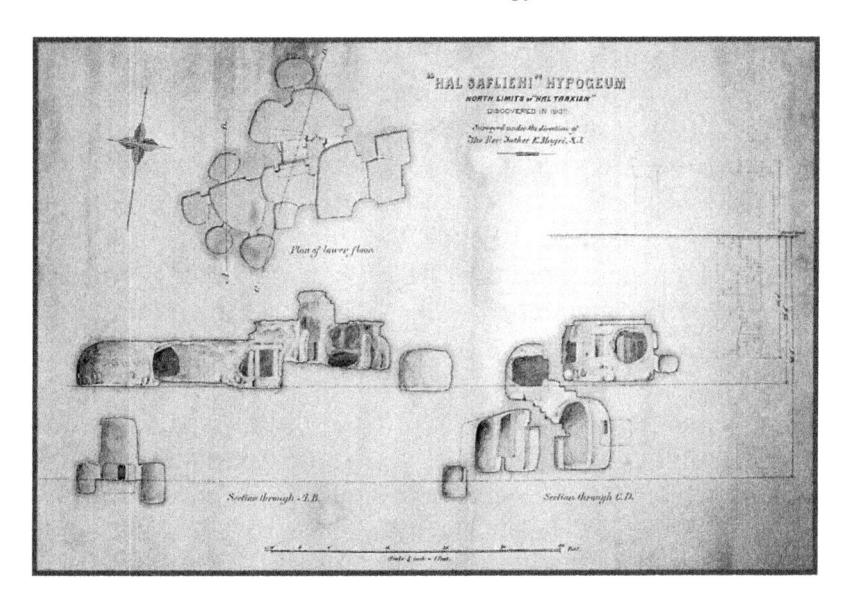

Plan of the Hypogeum at Manwel Magri's excavation

One of the chamber entrances leads through to the Holy of Holies and this is the passageway where an ancient bison-bull was once painted on the wall. Another area with a replica temple carved entrance including a partially corbelled roof, providing more evidence to add to the debate about temple roofing. From place to place are tethering holes usually near, or on the floor in front, of doors suggesting animal sacrifice or maybe some of these carved double holes were for holding wooden doors in place. The interior of the Holy of Holies is of a less high quality finish suggesting that a more practical usage takes place here away from public observation and it is from here that seven steps lead down to a Lower Level, an area of little interest as it appears that early work here was stopped in full flow when the site was suddenly abandoned.

Throughout the Middle Level there are many portholes, trilithons, orthostatic stones and chambers, all exquisitely carved and a couple with names that have grown around them that suggest a usage that can only ever be speculation. The Oracle Room is a small side chamber that takes the voice of anyone leaning in through the opening and reverberates it filling the whole level with amazing resounding acoustics; this is a truly wonderful and inspiring sound whether or not the chamber was used for this purpose by our ancient ancestors. The effect is only enhanced by the red ochre painting still present on the upper part of the Oracle Room with a wonderful spiral design. Another point of interest is a 2 metre hole in the ground that has gained the name of Snake Pit although there appears to be no evidence of such creatures in the Hypogeum and another theory that the pit could have been for votive offerings may ring more true.

A small amount of pottery from the Zebugg Period found near the entrance of the Hypogeum suggests that the site began use around 4000 BC and the collection of other pottery from across the Temple Period would confirm usage until around 2500 BC when this amazing period came to an abrupt halt at the time know as the Desertion. During the 1600 years of active usage, Zammit, by extrapolating out from a small sample, calculated that the site would have seen around 7000 burials fitted into the chambers by pushing back the older bones already present. It is clear that not every area of the Hypogeum would have been solely for burial and that some areas would have been for some form of burial rite and ceremony but as to the content of any such ritual we can only speculate. Maybe more information will be forthcoming from excavations at the Xagħra Circle, a similar underground burial in Gozo that has been known about since the 18th Century but still awaits much work to complete.

Kordin Three Temple

Kordin Three Forecourt & Façade

Not many of Malta's ancient temples were built in geographic isolation and Kordin Three was no exception as there used to be at least three monuments of this type grouped together on the high ground overlooking the southern end of the Grand Harbour. Unfortunately Kordins One and Two are now in a destroyed state but Kordin Three, in spite of taking a full-on hit from a bomb in WWII, still survives. At the time of writing this temple had been closed to public viewing for some years, but with the property now under the ownership of Heritage Malta, hopefully it will be reopened to the public before too long.

Kordin Three is now located in a heavily industrialized area that has built up around it and can be found by following the road from Marsa to the Three Cities and looking out for the mosque tower on the right. The site is on the other side of the road next to the church and enclosed by a high wall.

It is thought that Kordin Three was discovered by Dr A A Caruana in 1892, who carried out a first preliminary excavation of the site but it was not until 1908/09 that more serious work took place, this time by Themistocles Zammit and Dr Thomas Ashby. Then in 1953 and 1961 Dr John Evans and Dr David Trump took a further look at Kordin in order to effectively date the site by examination of its pottery deposit layers. It was found that the main temples dated as far back as the Ġgantija Period (3600-3200 BC) with possible further construction work carried out in the Tarxien Period (3150-2500 BC). The temple structure itself consists entirely of the softer globigerina limestone with only a quern found in the upper left hand apse of the main temple being of coralline limestone. Pottery remains were recovered from buildings that neighbour the temples which provided dates for these sections and many artefacts were recovered from the temples such as pottery shards, flint tools, a stone pounder and animal bones. Remains of torba flooring were found throughout the temples suggesting that the apse floors were laid with this substance.

On visiting and approaching from the main gate, the usual concaved façade that must have had some of its large stones repositioned, is striking, standing around its forecourt that unusually is laid with large stone paving slabs. There are two portal entranceways through this façade leading to two separate temple buildings, the one to the left, or the Western Temple, being the largest and of a typical trefoil design. The entrance passageway to this building is flanked by four large pairs of orthostats that have long since lost their overhead trilithons, or lintels, but the stone paving continues through and into the central court from which the three apses lead. A curious feature of the corridor paving is the presence of three cross slabs each laid on edge that would have caused anyone entering to stride over them.

From the inside rear of Kordin Three, showing the stone paving & trough

The terminal apse, opposite the entrance and the right hand apse of this temple are well formed and preserved with the usual curved walling still remaining to the height of two or three bricks in places. These two rooms are separated from the courtyard by low walls of upright stones with entrance gaps. The left hand apse is a little more complicated in that it has been divided into two by a wall that runs directly through it and with the southern portion being accessed though a short passageway lined with three pairs of upright stones. Two niches were found built into the wall in this section, perhaps used as altars. The upper segment of this left hand chamber can only be accessed from the central court and then only by striding over a long, narrow stone quern placed haphazardly in the opening between two upright stones. The quern is carved out of one piece of the harder coralline limestone to consist of seven deep sections that could have been used for grinding or storage.

The entrance to the second temple to the right of the façade is flanked by two large upright stones one showing carved tethering holes. These lead into a mainly ruined area where the remains of two apses are marked by rows of stone blocks, but it is argued that a third apse opposite the entrance could well have been part of the original building. At some point the stones of this temple have been used to build a lime-kiln making any real interpretation difficult.

Excavations have shown that the various stone wall remains around the main temple structure are from an extensive village that appears to be older as pottery fragments from the Mgarr Period (3800-3600 BC), were recovered here in 1961 by Evans and Trump.

The Tarxien Temple

Entrance portal to the Tarxien South Temple

The Tarxien Temple is to be found in the heavily built up area of Paola, not too far from the Hal Saflieni Hypogeum and easily accessible from Valletta by bus. The site could be thought of as a complex of temples that grew over hundreds of years making it one of the largest and most visually impressive of those in Malta. The site's various stages of development produced many interesting facets, some quite unique to Tarxien, that whilst adding to our sum of knowledge may also have the opposite effect of adding to the mystery that surrounds them.

The Tarxien Temples were discovered in the wake of reports from islanders that followed the finding and excavations of the Hal Saflieni Hypogeum in the early years of the 20th century. In 1913 a farmer noticed large stones under the surface of the land he was working and this began the excavations by Sir Themistocles Zammit between 1915 and 1918, with work being temperately halted during WWI. Thus this amazing monument was uncovered at a crucial time as a housing boom supplying homes for workers in the British dockyards would have seen the site built over. Over the intervening years, further excavations have taken place at Tarxien as various archaeologists have attempted to answer the many questions that these ancient sites throw at us; by Thomas Ashby in 1929, John Evans in 1954, David Trump in 1958 and the Museum Department in 1997 and 2001.

It was found that activity at the temple complex could be recorded from the beginning of the Temple Period (4100 BC), as pottery from this early period was uncovered. Building on the Temple structures then took place with the Far Eastern Temple in the Ggantija Period (3600 BC) and then the South and Eastern Temples in the Tarxien Period (3150 BC), with the Central Temple following later. They were then in continuous usage until 2500 BC, when the islands became deserted for a period of up to 500 years. During excavation Zammit uncovered various areas of human cremation from the Bronze Age, around 2000 BC, when an influx of people came to the islands from Sicily, Italy and further afield. The burials, found at various locations throughout the site, included grey burned remains and burial urns containing various funerary items such as ceramics and copper daggers and axes.

The exact usage of these magnificent structures is difficult to say for sure but from our modern perspective they appear to be religious in nature and both the large and small statues from the site, all of which can be studied in the Museum of Archaeology, tend to reinforce this impression. Also uncovered were two fragments, apparently from a model of a temple façade, that could have been used as a trinket or a design piece for the builders of the monument. Another interesting and repeating feature found around the Tarxien sites are the round 'V' perforated holes drilled out of the rock and probably used to tether animals or to hold wooden door jams.

The sheer size and complex nature of the Tarxien Temples leads naturally to its division into these four sections for the purposes of examination and explanation; the South, the Central, the Eastern and the Far Eastern Temples.

Passing through the small brick building that houses the payment desk, a minor display of artefacts and a shop, it is only a few yards to a temple courtyard that is not easy to make out except for the curved wall, complete with an ancient bench, centring on the Temple. This is mainly because of the laying of walkways, installed to protect the site from the day to day damage that would be caused by thousands of tourists walking through the site every year. At Tarxien these boards and handrails are well positioned and can add to the overall experience by providing height in places.

Taken as a whole the impression here is one of a site squashed in amongst a surrounding built-up area, but a little imagination can replace the buildings and walls with the green fields that would have been the more aesthetic backdrop in the Temple Period and the true magnificence and size of the temple complex is revealed.

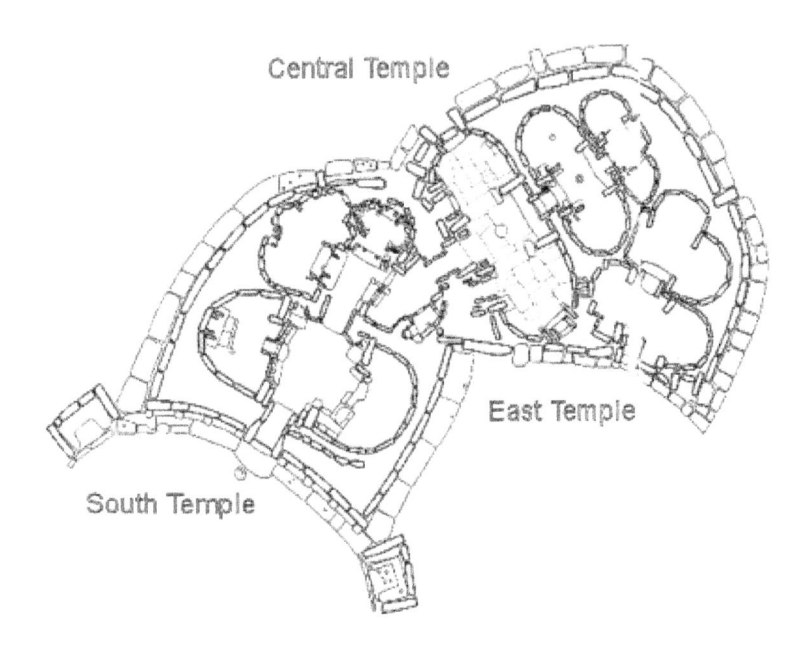

Plan of the Tarxien Temples

The South Temple
Tarxien Period (3150 BC)

Tarxien South Temple would have been of a symmetrical four apse design when first constructed in the Tarxien Period, from 3150 BC and then adapted over hundreds of years to meet the requirements and circumstances of the building's growing needs. Near to the entrance is a collection of enigmatic stone balls of various sizes around half a meter in diameter and of uncertain usage, although there is a theory that they acted as rollers to move megalithic stones into position. Also of note are the so called libation holes on the floor near the entrance, where drinks may have been left for the Gods, a water cistern and carved tethering holes that suggest a sacrificial nature to the monument, as it is here that livestock could have been tied awaiting the altar. On approaching the entrance the size and audacity of the Southern Temple is impressive but the two orthostats and flat lintel stone laying across the top to form a Stonehenge-like trilithon, have been reconstructed from concrete, an archaeological method that has thankfully been replaced with that of restoration whereby the site would be rebuilt as far as possible with its original materials. Much of the Temple façade has been rebuilt with dry-stone walling leaving a question as to the original design of the walls as it appears that all the original materials had disappeared by the time of excavation. Passing through the trilithon entrance the sight of the interior of the first two apses would have provided a real 'wow factor' as this was the most decorated area of any of the Maltese temples.

To the right of the entrance stands the remains of an immense statue that would have stood up to three metres high, dominating the interior space it would have definitely caught the gaze of anyone entering the Temple. This statue is often thought of as representing a Goddess, in particular the female deity known as the 'Fat Lady', statuettes of which have been found at Tarxien and the Ħal Saflieni Hypogeum sites. In fact there is no real evidence for this and close examination of the statue does not reveal any definite male or female characteristics so the person represented could have been anyone, maybe the person in charge of the temples. When Zammit uncovered the statue it had already lost its upper portion due to farming activity and it is now housed in the National Museum of Archaeology, the one at Tarxien being a replica. Again on the right, past the statue and a couple of low spiral carved platforms, facing the entrance is a stone altar standing on a decorated hollowed out stone plinth, again decorated with two levels of spirals, broken with a lower central bunged hole. Zammit found this to be full of animal bones, shells and flint knives, probably the left over deposits from ceremonies carried out on this block, standing on which is a small but elaborately designed niche constructed under a standard design from rectangular slabs.

The stone altar near the entrance of the South Temple

Opposite these in the left apse are found a selection of perfectly cut low level blocks all finally decorated on the facing elevation with pitting, spirals and animals again with the originals kept in the museum. Two blocks depict rows of animals, in particular 22 horned sheep and 4 other sheep, a pig and a goat (or ram). With these are standing stones in a haphazard arrangement suggesting that some form of statuary or other extra features are missing from the original display. Of particular interest are two megaliths near the central entrance to this apse, known as the 'Ship Stones' because of the inscription of various sailing craft and providing insight into Temple Period seafaring. A favourite theory of the author is that Malta was the location of a group of religious people who would provide blessings and protection for seafarers about to set out on hazardous sea journeys. The floors of these first two apses is laid with stone suggesting, as do the decorated stones, that this may have been a relatively well used, maybe public area.

Altar niche in rectangular apse

Carrying on though the two parallel concrete blocks of the central passage (that stand-in for the original orthostats), and into the second part of the South Temple, the other western apse has been generally rebuilt with dry stone walling. This may be slightly out of position but the small break in the wall with steps leading up to it appears to be in the right place as does a niche to the far right. Also apparently authentic are the two large megaliths at the entrance to this otherwise empty apse with Torba flooring. An altar niche in a separate rectangular apse at the end of the central corridor of the Southern Temple was the location of the remains of many fish and animal bones, probably the waste from ritual and ceremonial activity. This whole area was raised up to about 60 cm above the surrounding area by a stone platform with two rows of spiral carvings and the area was laid with stone floor tiles suggesting a type of stage.

Carvings of two bulls and a sow

The final opening, this time to the east, has been converted into a corridor through to the Central Temple with various small areas coming off it. A walkway to the right here leads through to a small chamber, made within the thickness of the wall, that has been covered and blacked-out apart from a small viewing area where with a bit of perseverance you can see wonderful carvings of two bulls and a sow, probably chipped out of the rock with a stone axe 5,000 years ago.

Central Temple
Later than the Tarxien Period

Encountering the large area that covers the first two apses of the Central Temple the immediate impression is that of a high standard of workmanship and an improvement to that of the Southern Temple. The orthastats of the apse walls here have been well worked and fit together perfectly, sometimes benefiting from an upper level of horizontal stones providing extra height and strength. Whether these formed the beginnings of a system of corbelling that may have continued into a roof will be the source of much debate whilst the remains of the hearth in the centre of the room may be proposed as evidence against such roofing as this would have required an adequate oxygen supply to burn effectively. Similarly fire marks can be found on megaliths around a huge bowl located in the left apse, which was incredibly carved out of a single stone. The large trilithon built into the wall next to the bowl may or may not provide more evidence of its use but either way this amazing container can be added to the list of Maltese mysteries. The high standard of workmanship can also be seen in the shaped stone floors that run throughout the area.

To go through to the next two, slightly smaller apses follow the central corridor, if the walkway will let you and over a low stone with two fine spiral carvings, (the so called Oculus Barrier), through the usual megalithic stone corridor and past two iconic stones flanking the entrance and with four carved spirals and pit-hole decoration (replicas). Another central hearth meets you here and the walls that remain of the two central apses are again extremely well formed but do note that some of these were missing and have again been reconstructed. The wall of the right hand apse runs close to that of the Tarxien East Temple and it is possible, but not certain, that a door through may have been present at some time when the building was in use. It is also possible that this wall had collapsed long before excavation because of a cellar found here from the Roman Period.

The huge bowl in the left apse

The final two smaller apses at the far end of the Central Temple are similar to the two previous examples. The dry stone walling in the apse to the right indicates a reconstructed area because of a loss of the original material whilst the orthastats in the left apse are more authentic. A central niche ends the main passageway at the eastern end of the Central Temple.

The walkway leaves the Central Temple through the wall boundary of the first right hand apse where a deep pit reveals one of the round stone balls sitting beneath a megalith, suggesting that it was used to position the large stone. Another point of interest here is the staircase that was built between the Central and the Eastern apses posing the question as to why anyone would wish to get to this higher level of the building; could it have been to gain access to a roof, or was it a viewing area? Yet another mystery to add to the overall picture.

Eastern Temple
Tarxien Period (3150 BC)

The safety walkway from the Central Temple leads directly into the four apse Eastern Temple where the first two side chambers are well formed and complete with tightly placed orthostats and Torba flooring. The general standard of finish is not as refined as the Central Temple, causing some to argue that the Eastern one was built first. The right apse of the other two remaining is also quite complete whilst the wall of its partner on the left has been replaced by the now familiar dry stone wall as the original was not found during excavation. This highlights the problem with the replacement method as up to date reports on Tarxien suggest that this left apse may have been joined to that of the right hand apses, second and/or third row of the Central Temple, thus forming a large space. The author would see one problem here in that whilst the workmanship of this whole area could have been carried out by the same set of stone masons, the standard of finish in the Eastern Temple is quite inferior and therefore different. It is also possible that this loss of an apse wall was a result of the same Roman cellar as that which may have affected the Central Temple, above.

Far Eastern Temple
Ggantija Period (3600 BC)

Situated east of the main complex, the Far Eastern Temple is thought to have been the earliest constructed of the four buildings, so it is of regret that most of the structure of the Temple has been lost with only wall footprints, mainly of the first two apses, remaining. It is thought that the original design would have been of a relatively small five apse Temple built out of small stone blocks not unlike the North Temple at Mnajdra, instead of the tall orthostats in the rest of Tarxien. Unfortunately, by the time of excavation, most of the above ground blocks had been removed, probably for nearby building after being uncovered during ploughing. Like most of the Temples the façade looks over a forecourt and in this case to enter the building through what would have been a trilithin doorway there is a step up over a row of shaped small blocks. The Corridor, running down the centre of the Temple was laid with stone flags, whilst the apses had floors of Torba. At some point and for an unknown reason, a pit was dug just off the central passageway at the level of the second apses.

Chapter 8

Southern Malta

A painted fishing boat in Marsaxlokk Bay

The south-eastern section of the island of Malta, in contrast to the heavily built up areas around Valletta to the north, covered in the previous chapter, is mainly farm land with various small towns scattered around the landscape. A quick look at a map shows that the centre of the area is dominated by the island's main airport in Luqa, with a runway of around

2.2 miles long, quite a size on a total landmass of only 17 miles in length.

On the eastern coastline Marsaxlokk Bay, the second largest on the island after the Grand Harbour, was favoured by the Phoenicians as long ago as 700 BC as it faced east towards potential enemy attack. It was these early Iron Age people who first built a temple at Tas-Silġ, overlooking the bay to protect their ships. The fishing town of Marsaxlokk itself is well worth visiting especially on market days when the stalls spread the length of the eastern sea front and the many bars and eating establishments are buzzing. Here the traditional fishing boats, the Luzzus, painted in bright colours with the 'Eye of Protection' on the bows, just finish off the picture. Further south but still on Marsaxlokk Bay the town of Birżebbuġa, again historically known for its fishing, has grown in size due to the Freeport and container terminal that can be seen as something of an eyesore on the horizon. The islands of Malta have historically been well situated for passing trade in the centre of the Mediterranean and this facility takes advantage of this to provide much needed employment and trade for the island. On the main road into town from the north are the ancient cave of Għar Dalam and the Bronze Age Borġ-in-Nadur.

The views out to sea across the south coast of the island are unparalleled and attract thousands of tourists to the Blue Grotto every year to dive in the clear waters or take a boat through the caves there.

Nearby, the two important ancient temples of Ħaġar Qim and Mnajdra are lying close together near the sea, overlooking the tiny and uninhabited island of Filfa five kilometres away and forming the most southerly point of the whole archipelago. This island that used to be used as target practice by the British armed forces is now a protected wild life sanctuary. This tiny islet was joined to mainland Malta in the last Ice Age and it is thought by some that the collapse of the joining land bridge has a catastrophic affect.

Birżebbuge, Silos and Cisterns

Birżebbuge, Silos and Cisterns

At Birżebbuge on the seashore of St Georges Bay, rising sea levels are encroaching on what may have been a pre-historic trading harbour that today is used as a handy bank by local fisherman. What remains is a collection of storage containers, that could have contained liquids or grain, carved and hollowed out of a piece of bedrock. Some of the rock here could well be fissured and so not suitable for water storage but they are in an ideal position for sea trade of many other materials.

A Silos at St George's Bay, Birżebbuge

This site is at the bottom of the main road into Birżebbuge, past the Għar Dalem and then Borġ in-Nadur sites and just where the road meets the waters of St George's Bay steps lead down to the flat rock bank.

Borġ in-Nadur Temple

Borġ in-Nadur temple façade

Borġ in-Nadur temple stands on a rocky plateau above St George's Bay on the main road into Birżebbuġa, with the entrance on a side street signposted 500 metres further down the hill from the Għar Dalam Cave. The site is closed to the public probably because of its disorganised state but private access can be arranged through Heritage Malta.

The shape of the usual temple forecourt cannot be seen as the land immediately in front of the site has been ploughed out although it would have measured around 22 by 15 metres. Some stones of the facia are still in place however and others have been repositioned. One upright megalith of the entrance portal is still in position holding up a broken capstone but a further large stone to the left of this would suggest that the original front of the site may have been much higher than it appears now. Passing through the portal entrance the layout of the original temple is not clear as many of the stones from the building were piled up to one side on excavation by Dr Margaret Murray in the mid 1920s, or during later occupation of the site. Enough of the curved walls of some of the side apses are still in position, though, to just about make out the ground plan of a four apse temple with a possible fifth terminal apse now not to be seen.

A Temple apse at Borġ in-Nadur

Somehow the semi-ruined state of the Borġ in-Nadur temple doesn't detract from its superb ambience that comes from its setting in open fields with views over the Bay below. This is a very pleasant place to visit!

The Temple has been dated from the Tarxien section of the Temple Period (3150-2500 BC) and it would have been abandoned for a long period at the end of this phase before the land around it was reoccupied in a section of the Bronze Age named after the site, (Borg In-Nadur Period 1500–700 BC).

A large wall of around 4.5 metres high indicating the extent of the village is still in situ and can be visited at any time by following a track up from the road through small agricultural plots. A 'D' shaped protective bulwark is also present but others walls and stone mounds can be misleading because of early haphazard archaeological digs carried out by A A Caruana in 1880. Unfortunately any hut walls from the Bronze Age village that were uncovered in 1880 and again in 1959 can no longer be seen as they were recovered after the excavations when a large haul of pottery shards were found.

A wooden Christian cross stands near the walls of the Bronze Age village indicating the place where a local resident, Angelik Caruana, reported seeing visions of the Virgin Mary in April 2006.

Għar Dalam
(Cave of Darkness)

Għar Dalam cave

The Għar Dalam cave and museums can be found to the right of the main road into Birżebbuġa, a road that has taken on the name of this important ancient site. The stone building that fronts the complex is easy to spot but the car park, being slightly before the entrance area, can be missed on the first visit.

On entering the building there are two separate museums one on either side of the Heritage Malta desk. To the right is a Victorian style hall produced by Dr Joseph G Baldacchino in the mid 1930s to contain a massive, if repetitive, collection of hundreds of bones recovered from the cave and displayed in wall cabinets. To the centre of the room are reconstructed skeletons of various specimens including a brown bear, hippopotamus and elephant. Since 2002 an educational style museum has been situated across the corridor to the old museum containing separate display cabinets each designed to explain various aspects of Earth and in particular Maltese science and history. Two excellent large oil paintings by Robert Caruana Dingli, commissioned for the Malta Pavilion of the Wembley British Empire Exhibition of 1924 also decorate this room with depictions of Pleistocene animal life and the Maltese countryside.

Passing through this area and back into the open air the view is of the Dalam Valley and as you walk down the stone steps to the mouth of the Għar Dalam cave the way is lined with an interesting selection of typical Maltese plants, shrubs and trees. The valley dates back as far as the Pleistocene Age around two million years ago when much of Europe was going through times of intermittent Ice Ages and warmer periods. The Maltese Islands themselves appear to have avoided ice coverage, experiencing instead an extreme wet era of storms and flooding that formed much of the landscape seen today. At Għar Dalam surface water seeped through the porous rock slowly dissolving it and forming an underground cavern resting above the harder coralline limestone strata. This space grew over time until the ground above it could not hold the weight of the surface water coverage and the whole thing collapsed to form the valley with two caves opposite each other being the original cavern. The cave entrance opposite is small with no great significance but Għar Dalam itself has proved to be of much archaeological intrigue and has revealed an enormous amount of information about Malta's distant past.

Carved initials of Giuseppe Despott at Għar Dalam

The first person to uncover interesting remains in Għar Dalam was Arturo Issel who carried out a limited excavation in 1865 and to his surprise found hippopotamus bones and impressed-ware pottery, from early settlers from up to 5500 BC, that was later given the name Għar Dalam pottery. Since Issel there has been much work with many digs in the cave carried out by John Henry Cooke in 1892/3 and other illustrious archaeologists such as Napoleon Tagliaferro, Giuseppe Despott (who, amongst others, carved his initials on the cave wall), Themistocoles Zammit, Dr Joseph G Baldacchino and Dr Thomas Ashby throughout the early part of the 20th century and many more since. Excavation work was halted during the Second World War when the cave became occupied by around 200 refugees of the bombing until they were removed by the British authorities in October 1940, who then used the area to store aviation fuel. Għar Dalam had also been used as a cattle pen until 1912 and this was probably when it's entrance was widened and a triangular stone just outside from this time would have been used to tether animals.

Investigation of the cave identified six stratified layers of remains. The lowest was 'Bone free clay' (125 cm thick), that had already been present before the cave collapsed. Above that is the 'Hippopotamus Layer' (120 cm), dating from 180,000 to 130,000 years ago and containing various animal bones. The 'Pebble Layer' (35 cm) follows and then the 'Deer Layer' (175 cm), dating from 18,000 to 10,000 years ago and containing many animal bones of this period including brown bear, red fox, wolf, bear, otter, bats and other rodents but mostly deer. It was in this layer that a number of human 'taurodont' molars were found in 1917 of a type exclusive to Neanderthal Man. These finds have led to much ongoing debate as to the earliest date that human kind arrived on the Maltese islands (see Chapter 1. Maltese Prehistory-Palaeolithic Controversy, above). Then is the 'Calcareous Sheet' (6 cm) which probably resulted from volcanic activity. The uppermost level is the 'Domestic Layer' (74 cm), containing the remains of farming animals such as cows, pigs sheep and human habitation from up to 5,500 BC including slingshot and flint tools.

Examination of the bones of the Hippopotamus layer provide proof of animals that walked the island in the Pleistocene Age having crossed a land-bridge from Sicily that had been formed after ice retreated and a lowering of sea level of around 250 metres. As the sea bed between Malta and Sicily is around 90 metres and that to Africa is considerably deeper this situation effectively ended a theory that animals had crossed from Africa as the span of sea across to that continent would have remained flooded. Some of the fauna discovered in the cave were unusual such as giant dormice, tortoises, lizards and swans, pygmy elephants and hippopotamus, all of which show the result of local evolution and adaptation to their new surroundings after being deserted on the islands when the land-bridge became re-flooded (see, Chapter 1, Maltese Pre-History, Formation of a Mediterranean Archipelago).

Stalagmite at Għar Dalam

Entering Għar Dalam is a little like wandering into another world with the electric light casting strange effects on the stalactites and stalagmites, the wall crevices and ribbing and down into the low central trench. A high boarded walkway takes you along and into the 80 metres of accessible tunnel with a diameter of around 8 metres and then an inaccessible area continues over the same length into the darkness. An interesting pillar to the right of the tunnel, detailing the various excavation levels, left for antiquity by excavators, reminds of the importance of Għar Dalam to antiquity.

Pillar showing excavation strata

Ħaġar Qim Temple

Ħaġar Qim Temple Façade

The views over the rugged cliffs and out across the Mediterranean, with the tiny islet of Filfa in the foreground, are stunning from the area of Malta's south coast where the Temples of Ħaġar Qim sit on high ground. Below and connected by a sloping walkway are the Mnajdra Temples situated on a coastal shelf with the Misqa Tanks a short 250 metres above. This important area can be reached by taking the south road out of the town of Qrendi, mainly through farmland, for around two kilometres.

On arriving at the car park Ħaġar Qim tempts from under its massive protective covering but this must wait as the first point of interest is the Visitors Centre. Here you can buy site tickets and take in the short audio visual presentation before heading around the display area that covers many aspects of exploration into prehistoric Maltese life.

Iconic view – the tall orthostats of the Ħaġar Qim façade

On approaching the main Ħaġar Qim site and passing through the security fence the usual flattened, oval shaped forecourt stretches the length of the temple and beyond and you are greeted by the classic view of the Maltese temples with the concaved façade of Ħaġar Qim with its four massive rugged and weather-worn standing stones to the left. It is these impressively shaped megaliths, amongst others, that would have indicated the position of the site and encouraged excavations as early as 1839/40 by J.G. Vance, who published a report of the works in the Malta Times in 1840 and in the magazine Archaeologia soon after. Further excavation work has taken place at intervals, in particular by Zammit in 1909-1910.

The 20 tonne megalith in the Ħaġar Qim wall

In contrast to the tall megaliths the remaining stones of the front elevation are perfectly worked and cut to fit with a row of upright stones or orthostats face on with two rows of horizontal stones above and a trilithon entrance breaking the wall centrally to form a short tunnel. Before the entrance two holes have been dug into the floor to produce a feature found at other Maltese temples that could have served as libation holes, providing drinks for the gods.

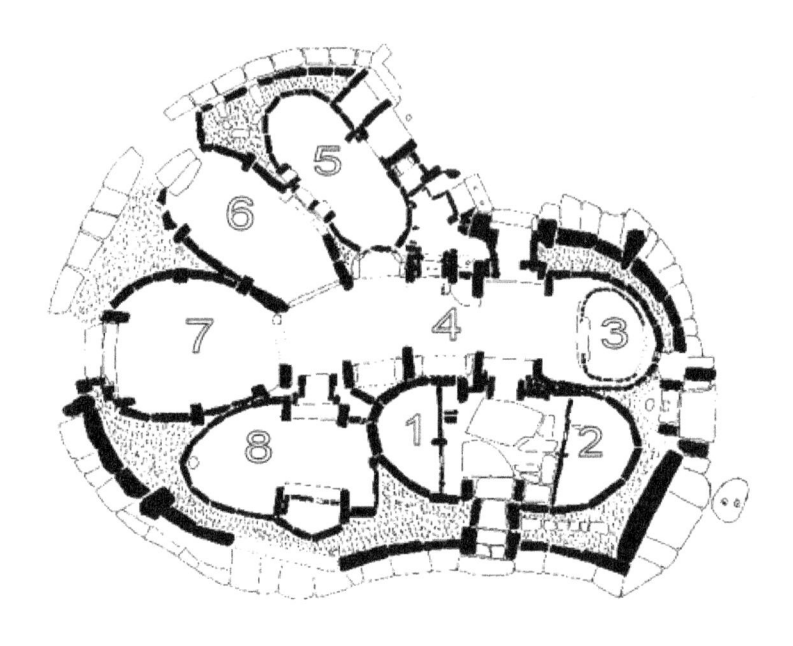

Plan of Ħaġar Qim Temples

This magnificent building was built entirely out of the softer and more easily worked globigerina limestone collected from a conveniently nearby outcrop. It appears to have been originally constructed as a four apse temple that was adapted by the addition of extra apses, or simply oval shaped rooms, extending from the left apse in the second row of the original temple. This whole complex was surrounded by a wall of huge megaliths with one outstanding example of 6.4m by 5.2m weighing 20 tonnes leading off at nearly a right angle from the temple façade to begin the northern wall. An external shrine is situated next to this with three tall megaliths and a low single stone altar but the wall megaliths behind it were replaced by a dry stone wall after excavation. An extra tall monolith of around 5m high stands at the rear of the temple with the added curiosity of having a hollowed out top from either weathering or human intervention for some unknown reason. Unfortunately much of the western wall has been lost and this complicated area takes some imagination to reconstruct in the mind's eye. What is clear though is that the open areas between the inner and the external surrounding walls would have been filled with rubble and earth to produce a wide and sturdy surrounding shell as can still be seen in places.

External altar area

Passing through the trilathon entrance and short passage, both of which are paved in stone, the sound workmanship of the first two apses (1 & 2) becomes apparent with standing stone orthostats to the lower portion of the outer walls, again beneath one or two layers of horizontal slabs. Both of the first two apses here are floored in torba and are partitioned off by a single row of orthostats with one to each side containing an upright rectangular hole that must have provided the only entrance. These so called 'portholes' may have had wooden doors, long since rotted away, as concaved areas around the holes and small tie notches on each side of the holes appear to indicate some sort of locking system. It was in this area that a stone decorated with pitting and double spirals was found together with a small alter like table with four sides, again with pitting and a flower or tree design. The original spiral stone is now in the visitors centre and the altar is in the Museum of Archaeology with replicas on display in the temple.

The Porthole entrance

Small decorated altar and double spiral and pitted stone slab

Continuing through the central passageway the apse to the right (3) is similarly constructed to the two on the front of the temple and a low row of stones suggests that this area was likewise isolated from the thoroughfare. There is a circular hole in the outer concaved wall of about 8 inches diameter leading through to the external shrine mentioned above. Could this hole be a way for those at the outer altar to communicate with a priest or priestess within, possibly through this oracle hole or was it drilled though to mark the place of the summer solstice sunrise?

The possible Oracle Hole

Unusually, the central passageway does not end in any sort of stone structure but instead has been left clear to form an outer doorway opposite to the original entrance. The Apse to the left (4) contains an assortment of altars but has become more of an access way to the additional built on chambers and it was here that a collection of 'fat lady' statues was found under the steps leading to chamber 8 and moved to the museum. Chamber 5 is of a usual two apse design with an entrance to the north through the external wall giving the appearance of a separate or twin temple very much like the Mnajdra and Ġgantija on Gozo. If this was the case then this could have been the original front elevation of the Ħaġar Qim temples with the impressive façade facing southeast being a later add on. Also following this theory chamber 6 would have been connected to chamber 5 by another central passageway and signs of such a passageway can be imagined from aerial design photos, even though chamber 6 also has open access to chamber 4 through the apse wall. Chamber 7 appears to be of a more rounded construction and whilst part of the overall complex is somewhat isolated with just one external entrance through the external wall. The final chamber, 8 is fully connected to chamber 4 by climbing three steps and through a portal entrance. This area is unusual as it gives the impression of having a single apse to the south as any matching structure would have to overlap with chamber 2.

Having examined the main area of Ħaġar Qim contained within the outer temple wall it would be very easy to imagine that this was the entire site but it is probable that there was significantly more building in this area in the Neolithic times of the Temple Period. The more recent builders of the sites protective cover were held up many times during the process of construction as various pieces of ancient remains were often uncovered whilst attempting to lay the holding bars. To the north of the main site are the remains of a four apse temple where whilst the right side has been mainly destroyed the curved shape of the walls of the chambers to the right that remain are enough to make the temple recognisable. A second building in the vicinity yet not directly connected to the main Ħaġar Qim temple lies to the east, between the fence entrance and the main façade. This confusing collection of stone walls with a curved front elevation does not much resemble a temple façade and it is a similarly perplexing situation inside the building with different shaped rooms that only very slightly could be said to follow the usual design. It is possible that this building may have indeed once been a temple that has been disturbed for its rock over the years, or perhaps badly excavated, today though it only adds to the mysteries of the Maltese Islands.

Ħaġar Qim and Mnajdra are amongst the five premier Maltese temples and are a must for any tour list and because of this and the sites importance as an archaeological site they were awarded the status of UNESCO, World Heritage Conservation, in 1992.

Mnajdra Temples

Façade of Mnajdra South Temple and forecourt

Having visited Ħaġar Qim, the Mnadjra Temples sit waiting on an a coastal shelf below and connected by a long man-made stone ramp that provides a gradual descent and an opportunity to take in some of the plants and wild life of this otherwise mostly barren area. The rock here is of both globigerina and coralline limestone and, unlike its sister site above, both types of rock were used in Mnajdra's construction. The views across Filfa Islet and out across the Mediterranean are wonderful and must have appeared so to our ancestors who constructed these buildings all those millennia ago.

There is the usual security fence and booth that lets you through to an oval forecourt of around 30 metres across and the three temple structures standing in a line are magnificent. Around these are a few outlying walls of miscellaneous and long disappeared buildings indicating that a complex once stood here, larger than the one now seen. Also amongst the pottery remains found around the Mnajdra site are pieces dating back as far as the Żebbuġ (4100–3700 BC) and Mġarr (3800–3600 BC) Periods suggesting that the temples were built on a site that was in use much earlier than the Ġgantija Period (3600-3200 BC) of early Mnajdra. The earliest excavation of this site took place in 1840, shortly after that of Ħaġar Qim and not long after the first dig that took place at Ggantija in 1827. Work on the Maltese temples has continued more or less non-stop over the years with more discoveries coming to light and alterations to the infrastructure intended to make the sites safe for the tourist industry and to preserve the buildings themselves. The most notable act of conservation is the building of the huge shelters over both the Ħaġar Qim and Mnajdra in 2009 to protect them from solar radiation, rain and acid-rain wearing, wind erosion and to reduce plant growth.

The first temple you reach, being the smallest and oldest to the right or north, of the forecourt is of a basic trefoil design and dates back to the Ġgantija Period. Entering through the south-west facing portal lined by two orthastats that are in turn strangely flanked by two others, you notice that whilst the torba flooring is original, together with a few of the larger orthostats, most of the walls have been lost. These were reconstructed from smaller blocks in 1952 to show the positioning and shape of the originals. The walls here are an outer stone skin with the interior filled to provide protection and strength. A small chamber was created in the curved area, opposite the door, that is separated off by two side orthostats positioned side on and three smaller stones facing to fill the front portion. All of these megaliths have a pitted design. The outer apses are simple but not quite symmetrical as the left arch is larger than the right, a misjudgement maybe of the positioning of the walls during reconstruction.

Central apse, opposite the entrance. Northern Temple

Although still of the Ġgantija Period, the South Temple, standing far left of the forecourt, was probably the second to be constructed at Mnadjra, with it's striking convex, eastern orientated, façade constructed of face-on orthostats above a well preserved bench and beneath one or two rows of now haphazardly positioned horizontal layered slabs. Before the centrally positioned trilithon entrance portal are so called libation holes in the ground and a well positioned rock with a dark crystalline strip running through it that leads though a short corridor of four pairs of orthostats with one roofing stone still in situ. On entering the inner area, the apse to the right (1) has walls of orthostats, two of which have oracle holes with below up to four horizontal layers of slabs that appear to narrow the roof space slightly, perhaps showing the beginnings of an actual roof.

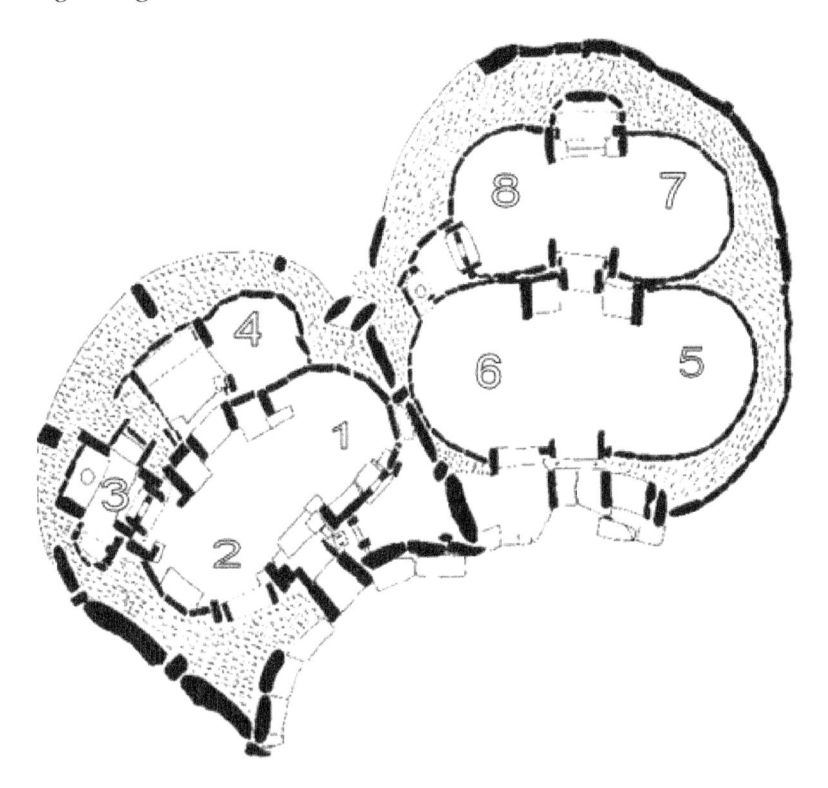

Plan of the Mnadjra Temples

A chamber, built into the thickness of the walls between apse 1 and the central temple, is accessed up three steps and through a porthole from the eastern part of apse 1, next to the main entrance and one of the oracle holes is also reached from within this chamber. To the right of the porthole entrance and within the side chamber is another similar porthole/trilithon that separates a small area next to the main entrance corridor. The second oracle hole passes through to another separate chamber that can only be accessed from the rear of the temple.

Apse 1 of the South Temple

Apse (2), to the left of the temple portal, is empty except for a porthole/trilithon entrance, flanked by two large megaliths and covered with pitted decoration that leads through to apse (3). At some time this small chamber was altered to contain three unusual double-layered stone shelf-like structures with central pillar supports.

The two side slabs that catch the sun at the equinoxes

It appears that the South Temple may have been positioned in order to fix certain times of the year through astrological alignments that catch the sun's beams through the central passageway at sunrise on the two yearly equinoxes and the solstices on pitted stone slabs to each side of the centre. A fine working model of this phenomenon can be seen in the visitor's centre.

Passing through the stone covered passageway to the rear area the central corridor terminates with an altar like table flanked by tall megaliths. The rear right hand apse (4) is set slightly higher than the rest of the temple due to its situation on the bedrock and its walls, although somewhat reconstructed, still contain some large original blocks. It is in this area that a clay figurine and other seemingly associated twists of the same material were found in 1910 during the excavation that discovered the uneven situation of the rock.

Façade of the Central Temple with portal entrance

The remaining Central Temple was the last to be constructed so it had to be sized to comfortably fit between the other two buildings but at a slightly higher level because of the same bedrock that effected apse 4 of the southern temple. Evidence of the stone work employed to level out the ground for building can be clearly seen in the heightened stone platform area to the front of the temple and above the forecourt. It appears that this temple had a form of porch as two broken stones are still present protruding from each side of a central doorway that, again unusually, had a porthole entrance, now with an upper portion missing. Strangely a second door was cut through the apse wall immediately left of this main entrance leaving the imagination running wild with the possibilities.

The frontal apses (5&6) are relatively clear and straight forward with walls completely constructed of orthostats topped off with two layers of horizontal slabs. The central walkway appears to be floored in torba, whilst the now unroofed passageway between the front and rear areas are paved in stone. A fine carving of a roofed temple can be found on a flanking megalith to the left of the passage entrance in the foremost position of the central corridor. There is a theory that an astrological alignment can seen around this central passageway similar to that in the Southern Temple and a model in the visitor's centre shows the winter solstice sunrise reaching the right hand megalith and at the equinoxes shining into the centre. There is a problem though with this light show as similar effects can be witnessed at other times during the year somewhat watering down the hypothesis, in the end it is up to the individual to decide and it is always good to introduce new ideas into this uncertain of subjects.

Passing through to the similarly clean rear temples (7&8) this central passageway ends in another terminal altar like the one in the south temple, whilst a small chamber with a porthole/trilithon entrance from apse 8, is built into the thickness of the temple wall.

Misqa Tanks

A Misqa Tank

The Misqa Tanks are large water cisterns cut out of a limestone plateau above the Mnajdra Temple and a fascinating continuation to a visit of the area that will take you off the usual tourist route. To locate the tanks turn left immediately on leaving the Mnajdra Temple and take the paths that head straight up the hill until the cross wall after about 250 metres and follow this left until the flat rocky outcrop.

Up to ten tanks here are quite obvious and of differing sizes from a metre in diameter up to oval openings of three or four metres in length. They are of uncertain and varying depth, although some are possibly up to three or four metres.

A Misqa Tank

The work carried out in digging these containers from the rock must have been immense but the result is a fine water supply that can be captured during the rainy season in winter to supply the temples below during the dry summer months. This ancient water supply is still welcomed by local farmers on the nearby hillside even today. In places grooves can be seen carved in to the rock surface that may have acted as drains to fill the tanks, although the shape of these lines has led to speculation that they may have formed some sort of symbol or sign. Dating of the cisterns from the Temple Period has been made from comparing the Misqa tanks to the one found during the excavation of the Hypogeum which defiantly carries this dating.

The views out to sea from the Misqa Tanks, over the Mnajdra Temple and the islet of Filtha, are wonderful and well worth the climb in their own right.

Tas-Silg Temple

Libation holes at the entrance to the old temple at Tas-Silg

Named after the nearby church of 'Madonna our Lady of the Snows', Tas-Silg is a massive and fascinating archaeological site located on a hill overlooking Marsaxlokk Bay, that stretches to both sides of a minor road. It is an extremely important and unique site being a place of ritual, ceremony and occupation with continuous usage for around 4,500 years. Excavations have been carried out here since an Italian group led by Antonio Cagiano de Azevedo and Antonia Ciasca, began searching for a temple of the Phoenician Goddess Ashtart/Astarte between 1963/72. This team discovered an unexpected much earlier temple from the Tarxien part of the Maltese Temple Period (3150-2500 BC) and carried on further excavations from around 1999 to 2012, together with a team from the University of Malta, who continue seasonal work on the site.

Part of the curved wall from the Temple Period

The remains of the Tarxien Period temple are difficult to make out after such extensive alteration work but a threshold slab complete with three libation holes would strongly suggest the entrance to an ancient temple. The Italian archaeological team located foundation footings of a four apse temple together with large megaliths that would appear to have once formed a temple façade. Then at a later date it was suggested that a larger complex of buildings from the Temple Period were hidden under the later masonry. The findings of the Italian group was confirmed by masses of pottery finds and the second largest statue of the 'Fat Lady' that appeared to have been purposely disfigured and reused as a building slab.

The Temple period site would have been abandoned, as was the rest of the island, around 2500 BC and left unused until Bronze Age settlers in the Borg In-Nadur Period 1500–700 BC occupied the site, probably using it as a village. So far the history of the Tas-Silg site mirrors that of the Borg In-Nadur Temple that also overlooks Marsaxlokk Bay to the south, but this changed with the arrival of the Phoenicians who settled on the island from 700 BC. It was these seafaring people that were to reuse the Tas-Silg site by constructing a temple to their Goddess Astarte. The Phoenicians settled in the town that is now known as Mdina and they arrived on Malta through Marsaxlokk Bay and this continued to be the harbour they used for travel and sea trade, thus making Tas-Silg, overlooking the bay, an ideal place for their God to oversee activities.

Firstly, the area that may have been the façade of the earlier temple containing a shrine, was either made symmetrical, or repaired to be in this way. An elaborate forecourt extension was added behind the shrine area surrounded by double columns that held a roof form a cloister and with a roofed entrance porch of single columns. The double columns of the cloister appear to have carried on around the shrine and again been roofed at some point.

Roman forecourt flooring & column positions

In this way an elaborate 'Greek Style' temple was created and continually improved right into the Roman area from 218 BC and by this time the site has also grown in size with many adjacent buildings being constructed around it, enough to cover a area at least four times that of the temple itself. It appears that alteration and maybe much of the usage of Tas-Silg ceased during the Roman Era but activity returned with the Christian, Byzantine Period from 535 AD when a square church was built over the Phoenician/Punic cloistered forecourt using the existing footings by building the walls of the church over the position of the previous columns. This 6th Century church consisted of a central nave with aisles down each side, an altar to the east, as is usual with Christian churches and with a complete roof for the first time. Behind the new church the original Temple Period building appears

Malta & Gozo - A Megalithic Journey

to have remained in position with only the addition of a baptistery in what may have been regarded as the most holy point in the temple.

The baptistery

This ancient place appears to have remained in active use probably into the 9th Century when, at a time of unrest in the Mediterranean area, it appears to have fallen into disuse with many of the stones of the building being removed and reused locally for other construction.

As can be expected from a religious site of such longevity the amount of artefacts found in the site is extensive, including many ceramics with dedications to the various deities of Ashtart, Tanit, and Hera, with associated red and black figurines. Much jewellery was also uncovered including earrings and chains and an amazing 276 coins were recovered from the baptismal, dating from a 200 year period from the mid 4th Century, probably left as votive offerings.

At the time of writing, excavations by teams from the University of Malta continue at Tas-Silg during the summer months. There are no plans to open the site to the general public, but an organised visit here is highly recommended.

Wied Znuber, Dolmen

Wied Znuber, Dolmen

The temples of Malta are a unique and fascinating study but dotted around the islands are a few remains of another time period, generally uncared for and compared with their larger counterparts, generally unvisited. These are the Dolmens, a style of ancient site that can be seen widely across Europe and further afield. It is generally thought that these simple sites are from the Bronze Age (2,000-700 BC) although little remains that can be dated and they could be older.

Wied Znuber is a fine example of a Maltese dolmen with a massive capstone apparently of coralline limestone measuring 3.8 by 1.6 metres resting on legs that would be considered quite short in comparison with most British sites of its type. In this respect Wied Znuber can be compared with the Lligwy Cromlech (dolmen) on the Isle of Anglesey in that unusually the chamber beneath the capstone has been carved out, although in the case of Wied Znuber this may only be by only a few centimetres.

It sits on a large flat limestone platform that must have helped in its preservation, with pleasant vegetation all around. As is so often with dolmen it is situated with lovely sea views, which in this case would have been much better before the area immediately inland became covered in factories.

The Wied Znuber dolmen is not easy to find being hidden away on a seaside headland in an industrial area behind what used to be the Hal-Far airfield. Luckily the old airport is marked on many maps so having found this the 'Playmobil' factory and fun-park is an easy landmark. From here follow the road from the 'Trelleborg' factory down to the 'Siegfried Pharmaceuticals' plant and take the obvious path onto waste ground to the rear where the dolmen sits.

Chapter 9

Mdina, Rabat and Western Malta

Mdina, 'The Silent City'.

The small western portion of Malta covered in this chapter is characterised mainly by countryside and farmland in stark contrast to the built-up areas to the east. The coastline is dominated by cliffs with terraced arable strips and wonderful views out over the Mediterranean. The major population centres of Mdina (the 'Silent City') and Rabat cover the summit of a high hill that can be seen from throughout the island. This was the first major settlement on Malta dating back to 700 BC when the Phoenicians landed their boats in Marsaxlokk Bay in the south and searched out a high place to build their city where they could keep watch over the island for any encroaching invaders. Mdina remained the major city on Malta, under the name of Melita, for over 2,000 years until the Knights of St John built Valetta after the Great Siege of 1565 when their town of Birgu on the Grand Harbour was ruined.

Mdina Main Gate

The ornate Main Gate into Mdina, built by Grand Master Manoel de Vilhena in 1724, leads over a deep defensive ditch into a the 'Cittá Vecchia', or Old City where the overwhelming impression is one of an enclosed stone environment. Immediately on the right on entering this walled city is the fore-courted Vilhena Palace, renovated in the Baroque style by Manoel de Vilhena. Within the palace is the National Museum of Natural History that has been run by Heritage Malta since 1973 to display the islands ecosystems through masses of wildlife displays from geology to preserved animals, birds, insects, fish, reptiles and fossils.

St Paul's Cathedral, Mdina

Further north into the city, St Paul's Cathedral stands on a piazza named after the same saint and again of Baroque style. The present building was constructed at the turn of the 18th

Century to replace the Norman construction that had been destroyed by an earthquake in 1693. An earlier Christian building fell into disuse under Arab control of Malta from 870 and rebuilt from 1091 after the Norman Conquest. The cathedral has a collection of fine paintings and decorated walls and the ceiling dome is magnificent. To the right of the cathedral is its museum that holds some priceless pieces including a collection of Rembrandt engravings, coins from throughout the Christian period, statues of the Apostles made from precious metals and many documents from the Inquisition.

It is not just the fact that most cars are banned in Mdina that gives it the name Silent City, it is the austere atmosphere created by a place with attractive narrow streets built entirely of stone without a break for any form of greenery or wildlife, but the result is also a city of quiet magnificence. Relief from the sombre mood of the streets can be found by climbing up onto the rampart walls and enjoying the views out across the island and out to sea.

Moving out of Mdina, Rabat was once part of the larger Roman town of Melita that was reduced under the Arabs to within the city walls thus cutting off this part that extends to the lower ground to the west. Today a central square here is dominated by a church dedicated to St Paul, built between 1656 and 1681 that replaced the palace of the Roman Governor Publius. It is said that St Paul was shipwrecked on Malta in 60 AD whilst under arrest and returning to Rome. He then lived for three months in the grotto that now sits under the church, where today a statue and memorial to the saint can be visited. A little down the road is a huge complex of burial catacombs that will be covered below.

Clapham Junction Cart-Ruts

A straight cart-rut at Clapham Junction

Cart-ruts are parallel grooves carved out of the surface rock found repeatedly across Malta and Gozo that appear straightforward at first sight but further examination of this phenomenon produces more questions than answers. The cart-ruts at the Clapham Junction site, so called because of the sheer amount of them and the way that many cross each other like railway points, are the largest collection on the islands. To find them leave Rabat and Mdina by the south road and head through Dingli, following the signs to Dingli Cliffs. This is a beauty spot where locals and visitors alike spend time taking in the sea views and it is well worth a visit in its own right. After driving along the cliffs for a short time and just past the

Madalena chapel, take a turn inland towards the Buskett Gardens and then a right and a visitors information board can be found at the top of the rise. The site is also marked on most good maps although these alone can be misleading.

Cart-ruts are mainly found to have formed into 'V' shaped grooves with the inner point measuring around 7cm across and the top surface up to 60cm, with the gauge between each pair of 1.41 meters, this being only 3cm less than the standard railway gauge of 4 ft, 8 ½ inch.

Point like cart-ruts at Clapham Junction

The cart-ruts at Clapham Junction and across Malta stem obviously from a different age and today's landscape appears to lay above it in that roads, buildings and man made ditches just cut through or over them. This poses the question as to when these grooves were carved. Can they have been cut by the delivery of stone to the ancient temples? This would appear unlikely as some of the blocks of stone used in these constructions were far too large for any vehicle and no tracks actually lead to any temples whilst only three lead to quarries. If not always rock then maybe the carts were involved in moving agricultural and sea products around the island as some of the cart-ruts run for quite a distance. The transport of water has been discounted as no appropriate vessels would have been available to contain the large quantity that would need such a vehicle. The transport of goods around the island does not explain the concentration of cart-ruts at Clapham Junction, but the grooves may have been produced by diverse activities in different locations. A clue can be derived from the fact that some cart-ruts have run out just before caves or at cliff edges above caves, could this indicate sea trade delivery and storage of some kind, or maybe the storage of marine produce.

As for possible dating it is apparent that the many grooves were in place before Punic tombs were cut through some tracks at various locations putting the start of the ruts before 500 AD. However there is evidence at the Borg in-Nadur, Bronze Age village of a cart-rut running to avoid a bastion wall, suggesting a date of 1500 BC. This would suggest a reasonable start point for the cart-ruts but when they stopped being made is a bigger problem. Just outside the Roman Villa in Rabat a cart-rut followed a road from that time period but by then surely wheels would have been in use.

Cart-ruts ending in rock cuts

When considering the type of vehicle that may have cut these grooves a wheeled cart would firstly come to mind, but as the grooves differ slightly because of wear, any wheel would have to be fixed extremely lightly so as to allow it to move within the cuts, or be pulled off. The sheer depth of some of the grooves would also require a very large wheel to allow the axle to pass over the central rise. Another more practical suggestion would be a slide-cart with two parallel poles being dragged along the bare rock. Wheeled carts could have been introduced later as the use of this invention expanded after around 500 BC. The problem of the wood wearing out against the stone ground could have been solved by the fixing of stone runners to the ends of the poles and this would also account for the great depth of some of the grooves. If a thin layer of soil had been present at the time this would have introduced an extra coarse layer that would have added to the grinding effect of the grooves, whilst providing a possible answer as to why the surface between the groves had not been ground down or even smoothed out by the passage of so many beasts of burden.

Malta's cart-ruts are a subject of study in their own merit, with so many of these intriguing pairs of grooves to be followed and examined all over the islands, but it is probable that we will never discover the whole truth of this now distant mystery.

The Domvs Romana

The modern façade of the Domvs Romana

The Domvs Romana was created following excavations by Dr A A Caruana after Roman remains were discovered during land workings in 1881 outside Greek's Gate, the traffic thoroughfare into Mdina, with further work being carried out by Themistocles Zammit from 1922. Although this area now stands in Rabat in Roman times, it as well as Mdina would have stood within the ancient city of Melite, the city having been reduced in size by the Arabs after they took control of Malta in 870. It was also the Arabs that built a Muslim graveyard of 245 burials over the Domvs Romana and interesting tombstones from this period can be seen on this site that is the oldest public museum in Malta after its opening in February 1882.

Entrance to the Domvs Romana is through a modern pillared façade and porch that leads to an equally recent rectangular hall, both of which were added in 1922, that contains fascinating displays covering the various historic periods as well as personal items found during excavations. Particularly noteworthy is a selection of terracotta theatrical masks but there are also many exquisitely crafted terracotta ornaments, glass and bone ware, from this site and others from the period. Also on display is a solid silver signet ring taken from the hand of a Muslim corpse.

The terracotta theatrical masks

The remainder of the museum is a reconstruction, from the 1920s, of what would have been a wealthy Roman home from the second and first century BC, with two side rooms overlooked by a main Doric peristyle courtyard, now roofed.

Each of these areas are floored with polychrome mosaics, thought to be the oldest collection in Western Europe and next to those in Pompeii and Cyprus, the finest. The courtyard floor has a three-dimensional design with a central image of two doves perched on the rim of a bowl, taken from a popular picture by Sosos, called 'Drinking Doves of Sosos'. The corridors are adorned with paintwork in the style of coloured marble and fine marble statues of an Imperial Roman family, including Emperor Claudius (Emp from AD 27) and his daughter Claudia Antonia (AD 30-66) and of a draped female.

The mosaic courtyard

An outside platform leading from the courtyard corridor allows viewing of other excavations that were begun by Zammit and shows the foundations and low wall lines from the Roman and possibly later periods lying to the west of the Domvs and east of the road.

St Agatha's Catacombs

The extensive network of catacombs beneath the town of Rabat are vast with a large part being the Heritage Malta controlled St Paul's Catacombs and it is recommended that a visit should start by taking in St Paul's and reading the section below as there are many similarities between the two sites. St Agatha's complex, with its entrance across the road from St Paul's, has its own history and unique features including a fascinating museum that can be visited before or after a guided tour of the catacombs. Here you will find an eclectic and impressive collection of archaeological finds from around the World, assorted pottery, artefacts from various historical periods and many religious pieces all under the authority of the Missionary Society of St Paul.

The historical back story is that in the 3rd Century the Sicilian St Agatha fled her homeland and Roman persecution to Malta, taking sanctuary either in the underground grotto that takes her name, or nearby. She eventually returned to Sicily where she died in a Roman prison.

Eventually over the centuries the underground complex grew into the catacombs and basilica church we see today adorned with frescos of the saints from the 12th Century and many more by Salvatore D'Antonio from 1480. The size of the area given over to Christian devotion has reduced since 1575, when a Monsignor Pietro Duzina reported many altars and today there are only two, the main one dedicated to St Agatha and a side altar, to Mary Mother of Jesus.

Moving further into the catacombs some of the graves still show the remains of early painting including one that had been hidden behind a covering of mortar that shows pelicans and roses with a covering frieze. Another has the words 'Before the Calends of September, Leonias was buried here' written in Greek. Perhaps the most remarkable area of the catacombs is a semicircular carved chapel of 275 cm across, that is surrounded with friezes and pillars and has a wonderfully painted altar.

St Paul's Catacombs

Carved ceremonial chamber with central agape table

The entrance to St Paul's Catacombs is on Bajjada Triq Sant Agata, just a couple of minutes walk from St Paul's church in Rabat. In 2015 a new Heritage Malta visitor's centre was opened and the amount of entry shafts was greatly increased allowing access to a much enlarged area of the 2000 square metres of catacombs.

The first rock cut tombs in Malta date back to the Temple Period although no such burials from this era have been found in Rabat. It was the Phoenicians from the 9th Century BC who, having created the town on a hill that became known as Melite and then Mdina, probably cut the first tombs here and with the growth of the city during the Roman period from the 3rd Century BC, the size of the burial site increased massively, a process that continued under Byzantine Christianity. At this time, when Melite was much larger and before it was reduced under Arab rule in the 9th century, the law required human burials to take place outside the city walls and the catacombs we see today are the consequence of this. In preparation for burial bodies would be embalmed with spiced oils before being wrapped in bandage, then after being laid in the sarcophagus they would be sealed with a stone lid that was fixed with mortar.

A multiple catacomb grave line

The resulting complex of interconnected and labyrinthine catacombs constitute the earliest Palaeochristian archaeological site in Malta, being connected to the story of St

Paul who is said to have lived for three months in a connecting cave under St Paul's church. After the Arabs were expelled from the island by the Normans in the 11th Century the catacombs appear to have been brought back into use for Christian burials together with other religions such as pagan and in one chamber a menorah is carved into a wall indicating a Jewish area. This inter-religious burial practice reflects a general tolerance of communities living in the Melite (Mdina and Rabat) area at the time.

Menorah indicating the Jewish area

The Catacombs were first investigated by Dr A A Caruana in 1894, who found a site that can be compared with many larger ones across Europe, but the Maltese example, not having significant foreign influence, is unique in character. Two large chambers were dug out of the rock that act as atria for the greater burial site where religious ceremonies and 'Coena-funebris', or funeral banquets, would have taken place. These halls contain carved columns, some with evidence of early painting and in one place a red figure can still be made out with a good luck greeting written in Greek. These large chambers also have low circular 'agate' tables or plates, of around 75 cm diameter, surrounded by a seating area that would be ideal for gatherings. Passageways head off from this area like a maze in every direction, lined with hundreds of tombs ranging from small indents carved into the walls, or loculi, for children, to various adult tombs such as window graves and forma graves for doubles and multiple lines of connected tombs for couples and families. A particularly interesting and repeated form of tomb are those adorned with fine carved canopies or baldacchinos, with cross arches. Also of interest is the tomb entrance block with carved surgical instruments probably marking the grave of a doctor.

Long after St Paul's Catacombs fell into disuse, they received another lease of life when they were used as bomb shelters in WWII and because of the constant low temperatures also for the storage of military equipment. Any visit to the catacombs today is fascinating and those cool temperatures can be extremely welcome in the heat of summer.

Chapter 10

Northern Malta

The 'Mosta Dome' church

The landscape of the northern area of Malta covered in this chapter is the most open countryside; characterised with farms, small villages and scattered towns. The northernmost point is the Marfa Ridge, just above Mellieha, where the ferry to Gozo constantly arrives and leaves from Cirkewwa.

To the west of Mellieha the seaside Popeye Village has been a popular tourist attraction since its creation as a film set in 1980, whilst Bugibba and Qawra on the south coast of St Paul's Bay are more or less dominated by the package tourist industry with the associated English and Irish pubs and cafes and night clubs. The seaside around this area is beautiful but the best beaches, like Golden Bay, are over on the opposite west coast overlooked by millionaires' apartments.

The area covered here holds some extremely important, if less known, ancient sites. Overlooking St Paul's Bay from the north are the Xemxija rock cut caves and tombs indicating occupation of the area since before the Temple Period and an ancient temple was discovered and preserved in Qawra during the construction of a modern hotel. The two further significant temples of Skorba and Ta' Ħaġrat are located to the west of Bugibba, near to each other on the outskirts of the town of Mgarr. From the Bronze Age the two dolmens of Ta'Ħammut and Wied Filep, can be found on the coast south of Bugibba and further inland to the west.

The south of this area is marked by the town of Mosta, the location the Church of the Assumption of Our Lady, more commonly known as the 'Mosta Dome', because of an incident that took place during World War Two. It was the afternoon of 9th April 1942, during a service when the church was full of 300 people that a German bomb crashed through the domed roofed and laded on the church floor without exploding. A bomb of the same type can be seen in a side room at the back of the church, placed there in remembrance of what is considered by some to be a miracle. The site is also interesting to visit because to view the dome itself that is the third largest in Europe with an internal diameter of 37.2 metres, with external rotunda walls of 9.1 metres thick. The Maltese architect Giorgio Grognet de Vassé designed the church based on the Pantheon in Rome, beginning work to upgrade the existing church in 1833, it was finally consecrated in 1871.

Buġibba Temple

Buġibba Temple

When the Maltese megalithic builders constructed their temple on the narrow peninsula overlooking what would become St Paul's Bay, the landscape would have been mainly deserted, accompanied maybe by just a small village or settlement now long disappeared into time. The setting here has since changed in ways totally inconceivable to the minds of our ancestors of 5,000 years ago as the area is now a thriving holiday resort surrounded by large hotels, bars and eating places. Amazingly though, the Buġibba Temple survived all this development by being preserved as a feature in the Dolmen hotel, Qwara, a somewhat ironic name with a dolmen being a totally different type of megalithic site than a temple and from another time period.

Access to the Buġibba Temple is though the hotel where the ever friendly staff will provide directions into the large courtyard next to a swimming pool, where the temple is overlooked by hundreds of guest rooms.

The entrance portal of the old temple is the most striking feature still visible with two massive coralline limestone megaliths supporting a capstone that has been relatively recently replaced to recreate a trilithon. To the left of the entrance two orthotats of the temple façade still stand, whilst to the right, one is still in position but leaning forward. The floor in the entrance is paved with stone and this continues through to where the internal corridor or courtyard would have been. A curved wall to the left of the courtyard indicates the position of an apse and a massive megalith resting on its side here was probably once the capstone of the entrance corridor. There are many stones scattered confusingly around the remaining area and it is difficult to make any real sense or form out of them, except for a wall to the right that may have been part of an apse on that side.

During excavations carried out by Themistocles Zammit and L J Upton Way in 1928, with further investigations in the early 1950s, pottery shards were uncovered that dated the Buġibba Temple to the Tarxien Period (3150 – 2500 BC). Two carved stone blocks were also found in the temple, one depicting two spirals and the other of fish, both of which are on display in the Museum of Archaeology.

San Pawl Milqi
(St Paul Welcomed)

The Church of San Pawl Milqi

Locating San Pawl Milqi is quite an easy process that begins by taking the road to Mosta from the four-way roundabout on the St Paul's Bypass and then on arriving in the town of Burmarrad, following the brown site sign to the right and up the hill. Apart from a yearly open day this site has been closed to the public for some years and private access has to be arranged through Heritage Malta.

San Pawl Milqi spans an extensive time period where excavations have revealed rock-cut tombs dating back to the Żebbuġ phase of the early Temple Period (4100 – 3700 BC) and the Punic Period (500 – 218 BC), with pottery sherds recovered from the Borg In-Nadur Period (1500 - 700 BC). A large villa and agricultural unit, mainly producing olive oil, was constructed during the Roman occupation of Malta from 218 BC. This complex continued to develop under the Byzantine (535 – 870) and Arab (870 – 1090) periods and then went into something of a decline.

It is thought that the earliest church to be built at San Pawl Milqi, was during the 4th century, but this did not survive for long and although another may have replaced it, no records have been found for this. It was not until 1616 that the present Baroque style building was constructed by Grand Master Alof De Wignacourt. An elaborate parvis was added around 1640 but unfortunately this was removed and lost during the 1960's dig, leaving the front entrance to the church three metres up in the air. The internal area of 8m by 3.5 m, has suffered from the removal of its flooring in order to investigate beneath, after which process new wooden beams replaced the originals. A hatch was left in the floor to provide access to the water cistern and/or vault that lies beneath, which is still under excavation.

Christian heritage has it that this was the home of Publius, governor and first bishop of Malta, and the place where he met St Paul after his shipwreck on the island in 60 AD. The account of St Paul's enforced visit to Malta is told in the bible, The Acts of the Apostles, 27:37-44 & 28:1-11, but whether this was the place in question or even if this was the correct side of the island is another of the Maltese mysteries.

At the time of the Roman constructions the Bay at Salina, to the northeast, that today contains salt pans and is otherwise much silted up, would have stretched much further inland,

Malta & Gozo - A Megalithic Journey

probably meaning that these early buildings may have been on the shore of this bay.

This site was first brought to the attention of the Maltese authorities in 1879 and was partially dug by Vincenzo Genech, a government architect and then excavated between 1882/1900 by AA Caruana, with the 'Missione Archaeologica Italiana', carrying out much more extensive work in the 1960s. More up to date excavations are still being done but whether Heritage Malta, with the financial responsibility for so many ancient and historical sites, will get round to preparing San Pawl Milqi for public viewing remains to be seen.

Excavation of the villa with olive press central

The Roman villa at San Pawl Milqi is a confusing site being still under excavation but earlier work records go towards revealing its story. Much of the masonry is of the 'Opus quadratum' technique, whereby large, well shaped rectangular blocks of coralline limestone, known as 'parallelepipeds' are laid together in courses and many examples of this type of work can still be seen. The central area of the building was the olive pressing, manufacturing or agricultural area, where a rotating olive mill known as a 'trapetum' (a fine example of which can be seen on the second floor landing of the National Archaeological Museum), was uncovered as well as oil presses, rock-cut channels and settling vats. Although the overall building complex is extremely large the residential section to the west appears to consist of only four rooms, with the walls painted plainly as decoration and with basic cocciopesto flooring (a type of concrete consisting of crushed stone, water and lime).

Inside the Underground vault

An underground vault, that can still be examined at the property beneath the present church and which may have been for the storage of grain appears to have become a water cistern over time, a valuable resource in a climate with such long arid periods. Excavations also brought to light a Punic inscription amongst funerary, votive remains that included terracotta masks and pots of a Hellenistic type from a period as early as the 4th century.

The property appears to have shrunk in size in the 9th century, during the Arab period, when a protective surrounding wall was built around the property and a corner tower was constructed to the west. It was during these difficult times that the property appears to have been abandoned.

Skorba Temple

Skorba's front elevation & entrance corridor

The Skorba Temple is on the edge of Mgarr where it can be located by taking Triq iż-Żebbiegħ from the town and then left onto Triq Sir Tami Zammit. The site is behind a square that appears after 300 metres on the left. At the time of writing, the Skorba Temple was not open every day so it is best to check with Heritage Malta before making the journey.

The Skorba Temples were discovered quite late and were only excavated in the 1960s, by David Trump. It was found at this time that the temples had been constructed on the site of an extremely early village, and pottery was recovered that was named after these dwellings. These pottery remains of Grey

Skorba (4500-4400 BC) and Red Skorba (4400-4100 BC) greatly increased understanding of the pre-temple period and finds from the Għar Dalam (5200-4500 BC) show evidence of occupation from Malta's earliest Period.

There were two temples built at Skorba, the first being of three apses to the west dating from the Ġgantija Period (3600-3200 BC) and a later four apse to the east from the Tarxien Period (3150 - 2500 BC).

Stone slab with Libation Holes

The usual oval forecourt that is a feature of Maltese temples has been lost at Skorba, as has the façade of the western temple together with the frontal (western) part of the right and left apses. The rear portion of these two apses still survives to one or two stones in height showing the size and shape of this temple. One large megalith stands to indicate the place where a trilithon portal entrance once stood and an interesting feature is the large stone paving slab lying before this entrance with libation holes, leading to a torba floored interior. Two further tall megaliths span the entrance to the third apse (central/rear) and between these stones are two smaller ones, both with two drilled security holes and these form a doorway. In the Tarxien Period four altars were built evenly around this doorway, inside and outside the apse, that have survived to differing levels of preservation.

Remains of the frontal, left apse of the Western Temple

The second temple to the east, constructed in the Tarxien Period, once consisted of four apses with a central niche, which was found quite late during Trump's excavation but it is now almost totally destroyed with only the low curved wall of the left, rear apse remaining to be seen.

Floor of a Red Skorba building

A further most important feature at Skorba stands outside the temple complex appearing almost forgotten in the garden or spare ground near the site entrance. Here are the floors and single wall linings of two oval buildings at least as old as the Red Skorba Period. These are amongst the oldest man-made buildings in Malta and it could be this multi-period feature that has earned Skorba the status of being one of Malta's UNESCO World Heritage sites.

Ta' Ħaġret Temple

Ta' Ħaġret Temple

The Ta' Ħaġret Temple is just a kilometre or so from its sister site of the Skorba Temple and can be located by taking Triq iż-Żebbiegħ, from Żebbiegħ into the town of Mgarr and taking the road to the left, signposted to the site. At the time of writing, the Ta' Ħaġret Temple was not open every day so it is best to check with Heritage Malta before making the journey.

The site consists of two connecting temples, the main South Temple with its complete trilithon entrance, with three steps leading up to it and flanked by the remaining orthostats and bench, is by far the most visibly pleasing of any of the smaller Maltese temples. It overlooks a still present forecourt that has unfortunately lost its oval shape and has a striking open backdrop of the valley and hills over to the south.

Through the entrance to the rectangular stoned courtyard

The entrance portal leads through to a rectangular stone-paved area of around 2.5 by 4.5 metres, with a slightly raised cobbled surround and it was in this area that a small carved model of a temple was found, depicting a roof of crossbeams supported on narrowed corbelling. This suggests that at least some of the temples may have had wooden beamed roofs. Three narrow doorways lead off this inner courtyard, one to each of the apses of what is a basic trefoil design temple with walls of roughly-hewn stone blocks with up to three high still remaining. The central apse, opposite the entrance, and left apse are well formed and of a basic design. The right apse, whilst still being in good condition, has had a hole broken through its upper portion to create a four-stepped entrance through to a second building. This smaller and newer North Temple appears to have been based on a three apse design with a fourth small apse created above the right one by the adding of a dividing partition. The reason for this extra room and to what use it could have been made can only be guessed at but an oracle area, as found for example at the Ħaġar Qim Temples, could be a possibility. All its walls remain at more or less the same height as the South Temple and are in a good enough state of preservation for the shape of the construction to be easily made out.

Model temple found in the courtyard

Excavations carried out by Themistocles Zammit in 1923 and 1946 and again in 1954 by John Davies Evans brought the Ta' Ħaġret Temple to light whilst accurate dating of the site was carried out by David Trump in 1961. The investigations found that both of the temples were constructed from hard coralline limestone and contained a plentiful supply of pottery to enable effective research. It was found that Ta' Ħaġret, as at the nearby Skorba Temple, was built on the site of a previous village dating from the Mġarr Period (3800-3600 BC). The large Southern Temple was then constructed on the remains of the settlement in the Ġgantija Phase (3600-3200 BC), followed by the extension temple to the north in the Saflieni Phase (3300-3000 BC). Slight and helpful restorations were carried out chiefly during the earliest excavations, in particular the main portal entrance to the Southern Temple had its lintel repositioned in 1937. More recently the Ta' Ħaġrat Temples became one of Malta's UNESCO World Heritage Sites.

Ta' Ħammut Dolmen
Dangerous Location

Ta' Ħammut Dolmen

Ta' Ħammut is a fine example of a Maltese dolmen if a little smaller than usual; in fact the capstone is around half the size of those of Wied Znuber and the main dolmen at Wied Filep. It sits on a rocky platform supported by a row of orthastats at each side and with one to the rear to form a spacious and full chamber beneath that may have been enlarged by some cutting into the surface rock. It is probable that Ta' Ħammut once had a covering of rocks that produced a mound but any traces of this have long disappeared. Lying to the left of the main dolmen are the haphazard remains of a second and a third has been reported nearby although this is not easy to make out.

Remains of the second dolmen

It is generally assumed that Malta's dolmens are from the Bronze Age, or Tarxien Cemetery Period from around 2400 BC and Evans in 1955 recovered a quantity of pottery shards from the period on this site during excavation.

To find Ta' Ħammut take the coast road/duel carriageway north towards St Paul's Bay and Bugibba and 400 metres past the peninsula road to St Mark's Tower turn left into Triq Ir-Ramia. This road can only be reached from the south so if travelling from the north turn round at the roundabout just after and retrace from the south. On Ir-Ramia stop after 300 metres just past the large house and the Ta' Ħammut dolmens are in the second field to the north, or on the right, over the horizontal wall.

The fields here are used as a shooting range so can be dangerous and the ground is very rocky and uneven but it is possible to get right up to the dolmen and when seen for the first time they stand well out from the surrounding rocky landscape.

Tal-Qadi Temple

The large supported Capstone next to the road

To find the Tal-Qadi temple first locate the four-way roundabout at the end of the St. Paul's bypass and take the road towards Mosta. On arriving in Burmarrad and just as the road separates into a dual carriageway through the town, take a 45 degree turn to the left onto a concrete surfaced road. At the T. junction, turn right and continue until the greenhouses appear on the right and stop adjacent to the last one. Here, opposite the greenhouse, a narrow unmade side street leads off and the temple will appear on the right after 50 metres or so.

The low apse wall and Capstone behind

On arriving it is immediately obvious that the whole site is in a state of ruin but some features can still be made out. The first stone that meets the eye is a large capstone supported to its inner by two orthostats and its outer portion has been reinforced by piles of stones in more modern times, probably when the area was transformed into a garden for the nearby house that has now become derelict. To the right are some extremely large megaliths that were probably part of the outer northern wall. Passing under the capstone, that may have formed the rear niche of the temple at the end of the inner corridor, an apse wall remains to the right to a low level and this helps to make out the position of its left hand partner. The central corridor area is no longer defined but a whole space with the type of flat stone often found in Maltese temples is present. It is thought that this building once had four apses but the shapes of the other two can no longer be made out, although there certainly are many shaped stones that could have formed these features together with the entrance portal area. To the right a set of stone steps descend to a lower part of the garden but these are a modern addition.

The temple remains were first discovered by a Civil Engineer by the name of Henry Sant in 1916, who as he was working for the Government reported the find and an excavation was carried out by Themistocles Zammit and Louis Upton-Way, in 1926. A survey of the Tal-Qadi temple site then followed in 1952.

The excavation found that the temple, that may have been orientated east-west, was in use from the Ġgantija Period (3600 – 3200 BC) and through to the Tarxien Period (2400 – 1500 BC), as pottery shards were uncovered from periods right through this time scale. Another most interesting find from this temple was a cracked globigerina limestone slab depicting what appears to be a type of star map or possibly a calendar, with five star sections and a crescent moon in the centre. This artefact can now be seen in the National Museum of Archaeology in Valletta.

The area around the Tal-Qadi temple appears to have once been developed and some of the houses have more recently been renovated and reoccupied and the greenhouse business appears quite busy. This rural scene may have looked extremely different in the Temple period, when Salina Bay would have stretched much further inland and probably to this point, before it became silted up and dried out. This temple may have, therefore, have been situated on the seashore.

Wied Filep Dolmens

Wied Filed Dolmen A

Wied Filed A is probably the best preserved and most visually pleasing of the Maltese dolmen. It stands 1.5 metres high with a massive capstone of around 4 by 1.7 metres with a depth of 60 cm resting on only three short squared off boulders with another couple of packing stones. Wied Filep B would appear even more spectacular than it does if it was not overshadowed by its near neighbour and it has much merit in its own right. This dolmen has a capstone of around 3 metres in length and impressively stands on just two substantial supporting blocks. As is usual for Maltese dolmen both stand on a ground of level stone and here a square stone enclosure has been constructed to surround the site but with an entrance gap.

Wied Filed Dolmen B

To locate Wied Filep take the 'Triq il-Fortizza Tal-Mosta' road towards Għargħur, north of Mosta, with a deep valley to the left. From the junction where the bridge heads off to the left continue for 500 metres as the road curves to the right. The dolmen are inside the square stone enclosure up on the bank, by the side of the road, on the right. Over to the left is a stone quarry that has produces huge white cliffs and there are houses to the right.

Xemxija Trail, Menhir and Caves

Xemxija Menhir

Above the seaside residential and holiday town of Xemxija a short, pleasant and extremely interesting walk takes the explorer through a rugged landscape complete with a treasure trove of historical and ancient caves. To reach the point where the path leaves the road take the coast road that runs along the land point at the end of St Paul's Bay, in the direction of Xemxija, then immediately after following the water line to the right and on entering Xemxija town, take the difficult left turn to face back in nearly the original direction and climb the steep hill. At the Porto Azzurro Hotel turn right and continue climbing and the trail heads off to the left where a small painted stone pillar indicates the direction just before the road takes a sharp bend to the right into a residential street.

Cave of the Galley and the Galleon Carving

The first man-made ancient site you encounter is a single menhir to the right of the path after about 100 metres, standing as if to indicate the perimeter point of this ancient place. It's uncertain when this stone was put into position, whether the Neolithic or Bronze Age but over the years this fine limestone post has been severely weather-worn creating that characteristic gnarled appearance.

Continuing along the path as it winds the short way up the hill there are caves hiding in both directions accessed by narrow tracks. Entered through small stone doorways these caverns, carved out of the solid bedrock, are unexpectedly spacious and have been put to a variety of uses down through the centuries.

Roman drainage at the path edge

One of the first is the 'Cave of the Galley', probably dating back to the island's Neolithic Age up to 5,200 BC, when it would have been used as a place of interment probably right through to Roman times. More recently this large space would have been used as a human home and possibly a place of refuge for a sea farer who may have carved the depiction of a sailing galleon of the type in use from the 16th to the 18th centuries that adorns a flat slab of rock near the entrance.

Roman Apiary

Another remarkable cave structure is the 'Roman Apiary' with its striking man-made flat exterior frontage, with rows of arched holes and two central doorways, that contrast greatly with the rough cave-like interior. This would have been used to house a swarm of bees for the production of honey in the Roman and Punic period, from as far back as 500 BC, when there would have been a collection of such units. The 'Rustic Apiary', above, is another bee- keeping structure that contrasts greatly in style to its Roman neighbour mainly in its rougher construction that blends in much more with its natural surroundings. It is thought that this cave would have had various periods of usage beginning as a burial area in the Neolithic and Bronze Age, followed by a place of human dwelling and then for farming such as honey production and then a cool place for hay storage and maybe other crops. It is also probable that all these caves were used as shelters during the terrible bombing during the Second World War.

The Old Carob Tree

The carob has always been a ready and important supply of nectar for bees so it is of no surprise that such a tree is to be found in this area, but the one that spreads its many branches from its huge girth of around 7.25 meters in circumference, is known as 'The Old Carob Tree'. This wonderful old man is thought to be the oldest on the islands and that it has been growing here for over 1,000 years.

To stand high up within this complex of age-old caves and looking out over the island and out to sea, cannot fail to bring to mind that others have stood in this place for thousands of years.

From here it is only a little further along the path and up to the plateau where ancient tombs can be found, but this is covered in the next section, 'Xemxija Rock-cut Tombs'.

The Old Carob Tree

Oh Carob Tree
So gnarled and so dishevelled
Who known how many events
Throughout your life
You had to witness
For our forefathers you
Were worth your weight in gold
And till this day
You steal our hearts
Reigning in beauty

Frans Scerri

Xemxija Rock-cut tombs
(Continues from the previous section, 'Xemxija Trail, Menhir and Caves'.)

Xemxija Phoenician/Punic tomb

Just above the caves discussed in the previous section and a little further along the ancient trail is a barren rocky plateau that was used as a place of burial as long ago as the Neolithic Period. To locate this area, take the well-worn path off to the right at the top of the rise and leave the main track to head off into the distance.

The first burial reached is a rare Phoenician/Punic tomb (circa 500 BC), that was probably adapted from a much earlier site similar to the others nearby. The upper part consists of a deep rectangular recess carved out of the bare rock, with an upper opening of around 2.2m by 1m, that would once have been covered with a huge stone slab. A small rectangular hole in the lower part of one of the narrow sides leads through to the two adjacent burial apses of the original tomb.

Openings to the ancient caves

The path soon passes between a reconstructed old style drystone farmers hut and a cave, that served as a human dwelling possibly from as early as Punic times right up to the 1930s. These early homes would have maintained a steady temperature, providing protection from the hot sun in summer whilst maintaining some warmth in winter. This large cave is divided into sections by rubble wall partitions that would have enabled those living here to separate human habitation from livestock storage. Maintaining a water supply would have been a vital part of ancient life and a resourceful system was devised here to collect the rain from the cave roof and direct it through narrow channels and ducts into a carved well.

Storage silo and cistern

A large silo nearby, again carved into the bedrock, would have been originally used for the storage of grain before it was converted into a water cistern at an unknown time in history.

The round opening would have had a fitting stone cap and the slots carved into the rim, leading into the cistern would have been cut to ensure that water would drain inward.

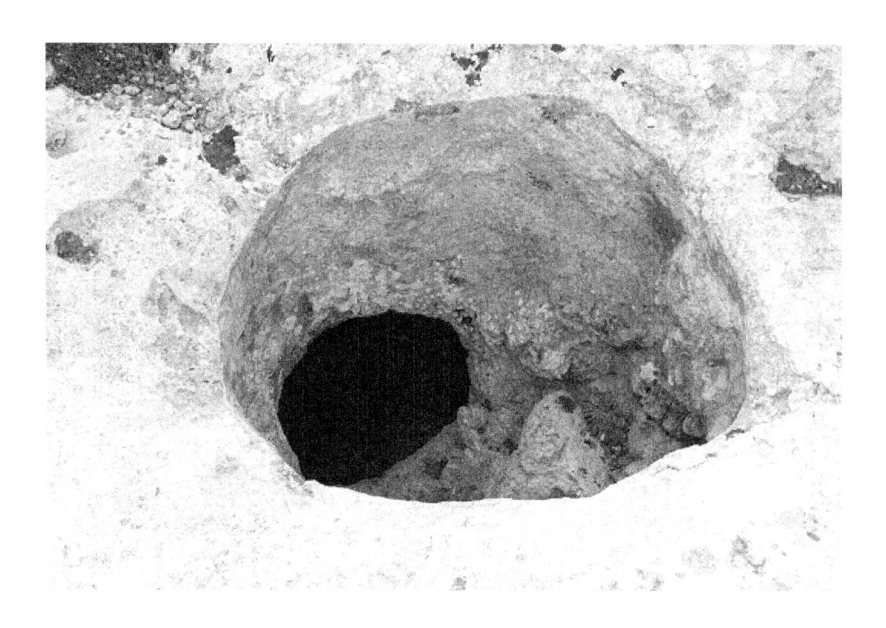

Rock-cut tomb showing the shaft leading to the chambers

Towards the end of this track on a flat, if uneven, coralline limestone outcrop just before reaching the road and housing, is a fine collection of six rock-cut tombs each indicated by a stone marker. These ancient burial places date back to the early part of the island's Neolithic Period, generally timed as after 4100 BC and to have been a precursor to the later temples which share the lobed shape of the rock-cut tombs inner chambers.

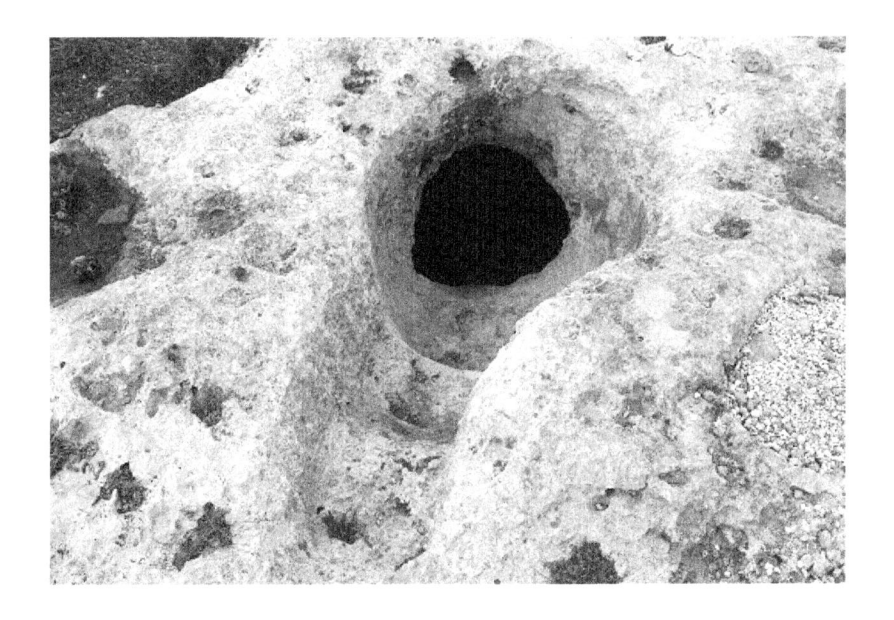

Rock-cut tomb with entrance steps

As with other such sites on Malta each of the tombs here consist of a vertical shaft leading to one or more oval shaped burial chambers. The deceased would be placed on the flat floor of a chamber in the foetal position together with grave goods to accompany them into the afterlife. In time bones would be moved to the sides as other bodies were placed within the chambers. Removable stone slabs would be shaped to fit the tomb entrance holes that in some cases had a carved lip surrounding the openings. Whilst sticking to the basic design, the tombs at Xemxija differ in size and the number of tombs, in one case up to five and in another, steps had been carved to allow entry into the downward shaft. (see also Chapter 1. 'Early Neolithic Period').

During excavation in 1955, John Evans found pottery shards and axe amulets mainly from the Ggantija Period (3600 – 3200 BC) and others from the later Tarxien Period (3150 – 2500 BC), whilst other remains dated from the Borg In-Nadur Period (1500 – 700 BC), suggest that the tombs had been reopened as late as the Bronze Age.

This collection of ancient sites, which also extends to a length of cart-ruts that can be searched out beneath the foliage nearby, suggest that a large population lived on this stone plateau in pre-historical times. Maybe it is somewhat ironic that modern day housing development has recently made its way up the hillside adjacent to this ancient landscape and the name of the nearest road is 'Triq il-Preistorja', (The Prehistoric Road).

Chapter 11

The Island of Gozo

A view of Gozo's ancient fortified Citadel

The island of Gozo lies 5km (3.1 miles) north-west of Malta and is best reached by a frequent 25-minute picturesque ferry journey that runs between Ċirkewwa, past the smaller island of Comino to Mġarr harbour on the south-east coast of Gozo. On arrival the differences between the two islands soon become apparent and there is a real feeling of having moved back in time. As of 2014 the population of Gozo was 37,342 with a density of 557 people per sq km (1,443 sq miles), compared with that of Malta, 1,410 sq km (4,077 sq miles). the island is also much smaller than Malta with a length of 14 km (8.7 miles) and a width of only 7.25 km (4.5 miles) and it has a much more rural feeling.

Gozo's main town of Rabat, to the centre of the island, has also been known as Victoria since 1887 when it was renamed by the British in remembrance of Queen Victoria's Golden Jubilee and a visit here is essential whilst on the island. The restaurants on Independence Square provide an ideal place to sit and take in the atmosphere of this friendly mini-metropolis before heading up the nearby flat top hill to the ancient Citadel. This area was first fortified in the Bronze Age and redeveloped many times throughout history and a walk on the ramparts provides panoramic views across the island. The main places of interest whilst in the Citadel include the Cathedral of the Assumption, the Folk Museum, the Nature Museum, the Old Prison and the Museum of Archaeology.

The island's major ancient monuments are the Ġgantija Temples and the Xagħra Circle, both situated on the plateau of the same name. Also in Xagħra is a windmill dating back to 1724, when it was constructed by Grand Master Manoel de Vilhena and overlooking Ramla Bay is the Calypso's Cave, a site mentioned in folk lore. It is said on Gozo that the island is the Ogygia that Homer refers to in his 'The Odyssey' and that the cave is where the beautiful nymph Calypso, daughter of Atlas, imprisons Odysseus for seven years in an attempt to force him to marry her. Many, though, also associate Ogygia with the lost Atlantis, that was to be found beyond the Pillars of Hercules, probably Gibraltar, as another name for Atlas is in fact Atlantis. The other smaller sites of Qala Menhir and the Ta' Ċenċ Dolmen are also significant and are covered below.

Gozo has more to offer than its fascinating historical monuments, and most people visit the island to take in its old world charm and beautiful Mediterranean coastlines. The most popular holiday resort is the old fishing village of Marsalforn, on the north coast, that has all the usual holiday facilities including a sandy beach, whilst the beach at Ramla bay, a little to the east, is considered to be the best in the archipelago. The resort of Xlendi, on the south-west coast, is situated at the inward end of a bay where high cliffs tower over the blue sea and the pleasant restaurants on the shore. On the west coast Dwejra is an area of outstanding natural beauty, where the Azure Window, a huge natural archway has formed in the limestone by sea erosion and nearby the Inland Sea is partially surrounded by cliffs that allow the sea to flood in through a cave tunnel.

The Gozo Museum of Archaeology

As would be expected, Gozo's Archaeological Museum is a much smaller version than its counterpart in Malta as it holds artefacts collected from this much smaller island. It can be found in the ancient citadel, situated in a fine two storey 17th century town house known as 'Casa Bondi', that was refurbished and restored in 1937 by Sir Harry Charles Luke (Lieutenant Governor 1930 – 1938). The property first became a museum in 1960 and was then dedicated as the archaeological museum in 1986.

The museum displays are divided into the three basic areas of Prehistory, Classical and Medieval, and Early Modern Periods. The first area encountered, just past the entrance desk, is the prehistoric, which itself is separated into the Neolithic, Temple and Bronze Age Periods. The various items here, fashioned from pottery, stone, bone or clay are displayed as if to study how the people of these times would make use of the available resources to survive day to day, collecting food, building homes, carrying out religious and burial activities and demonstrating their art. Many of the artefacts from these time periods that were recovered from the Ġgantija Temples and the Xagħra Circle have now been removed from the Gozo museum and can be seen in the Interpretation Centre at the Ġgantija Temples.

Moving to the second floor the Classical area is subdivided into Phoenician/Punic, Roman and

Medieval, where, as above, the displays of jewellery, marble statues, coins, glass containers and terracotta burial urns go some way to bring these periods to life. Of particular interest is the Islamic Majmuna Stone, a marble tombstone of a Muslim girl named Majmuna who passed away on the island on March 21st 1127. The historian Giovanni Bonello stated that the stone is 'the only spectacular visual relic of the Islamic presence in Malta' and whilst there are Roman markings on the reverse of the piece, indicating reuse, the beautiful Kufic Arabic inscription on the front reads:

'In the name of Allah, the merciful and compassionate. May He be propitious to the Prophet Muhammad and to his followers and grant them eternal salvation. God is great and eternal and He has decreed that his creatures should perish. Of this the prophet of Allah bears witness. This is the tomb of Maymūnah, daughter of Hassān, son of 'Ali al-Hudali, known as Ibn as-Susi. She died – Allah's mercy be upon her – on Thursday 16th day of the month of Sha'ban in the year 569, professing that there is only one God who has no equal. Look around you! Is there anything everlasting on earth; anything that repels or casts a spell on death? Death robbed me from a palace and, alas, neither doors nor bolts could save me. All I did in my lifetime remains, and shall be reckoned. Oh he who looks upon this tomb! I am already consumed inside it, and dust has settled on my eyes. On my couch in my abode there is nothing but tears, and what is to happen at my resurrection when I shall appear before my Creator? Oh my brother, be wise and repent.'

The displays then complete with exhibits from the Early Modern Period that leads right up to the arrival of the Knights of St John in 1530.

Ġgantija Temples

The rear wall of the Ġgantija Temples

The Ġgantija Temples could be considered as the premier site on the island of Gozo and in the same category as the larger temples on Malta, such as Ħaġar Qim, Mnajdra and Tarxien. Ġgantija consists of two large freestanding temple buildings contained within a massive boundary wall, standing on the Xagħra plateau, an area of land that it shares with the Xagħra Circle, another important site that is covered below. Being well signposted the temples are not difficult to find and if arriving on the island by ferry from Malta, they are off to the north of the road from the port of Mgarr to Victoria.

On arriving at the Ġgantija Temples, you are firstly guided into an 'Interpretation Centre', where the various sections contain fascinating collections of figurines, pottery and other artefacts gathered from the Xagħra Circle and other ancient sites around Gozo. This is not just a regular museum though, as the various display areas of the centre effectively tell the story of the island's early settlers and stone builders. This includes the local folklore suggesting that these prehistoric masons were a race of giants as the Maltese translation of the name Ġgantija indicates (Maltese - Ggant). More precisely it is said that it was the giantess Sansuna who build the temples in one day whilst carrying her human baby under her arm, balancing the megaliths on her head and living on a diet of broad beans.

From the Interpretation Centre a raised walkway leads down to the temples following a path initially to the rear of the site and the magnificent boundary wall, which in itself is one of the most impressive sights on the Maltese islands. The wall was built using megaliths of the tough coralline limestone, with some massive examples of up to 6 metres in length and weighing over fifty tonnes, raising the height of the wall to over 6 metres. A method of construction known as 'long and short work', whereby the main megalith blocks were laid intermittently side on and edge on was employed, which tied the wall together. The spaces between this outer boundary and the inner temple walls were then filled with rubble providing extra stability. Another building technique that is generally employed throughout this and other temples is the use of larger upright orthostats to the lower portion of a wall, with smaller blocks, laid horizontally used for the higher levels.

The forecourt area to the front of the temples stretches across the whole structure and is estimated to be over 30 metres in length, an area that would have provided a meeting space for hundreds of people to gather. As the temples are located on the edge of the plateau the forecourt is supported and raised by a terrace wall and beyond is a panoramic view, through a row of palm trees, across the valley and out over the island.

Long and short work of the perimeter wall

Facing southeast onto the forecourt are the convex façades of the two temples with a collapse to the main wall between the two entrances which appears to have occurred well before the site was uncovered and possibly millennia ago. It is a pity that this unfortunate pile of masonry could not be tidied up in some way as it has a detrimental aesthetic effect on the overall frontage to the temples that must have once been a spectacular sight.

*Temple façade showing the central collapse
and the massive wall to the right*

The South Temple is the largest of the two and was the first one to be constructed around 3600 BC, in what became known as the Ġgantija Period. The entrance to this five apse building is dominated to its left by a massive wall of over seven metres high, held into its original position by scaffolding. The entrance itself is flanked by two large Globigerina limestone orthostats, with definite upper groves that would once have housed a capstone to complete the usual trilithon portal thoroughfare. A vertical row of circular holes have been carved into orthostats to each side of the inner portal area that would probably have been used to hold wooden crossbeams that in turn may have supported a dividing slab. An examination of the Ġgantija temples will reveal repeated examples of blocking and tethering holes, that are a feature of most sites of this type.

Wall of the South temple central apse with upper corbelling

The passage that leads through this entrance is paved in slabs of coralline limestone that lead right through to the central apse at the far end of the temple. All the internal walls of the apses were constructed using blocks of this hard stone, which could go some way to explain its relatively good condition after five and a half thousand years. In the central apse in particular the height of the walls has been maintained well enough to make out the slight corbelling to the top, suggesting some sort of roofing. Although it is doubtful that the structure would have held stone, wooden cross beams, long disappeared, may have been used. Today the internal structure to either side of this apse is held in position by scaffolding, again an eyesore, but surely an essential one. The other four apses, branching off in two pairs along the corridor, with the two nearest to the entrance being the smallest, also have impressively high external block walls.

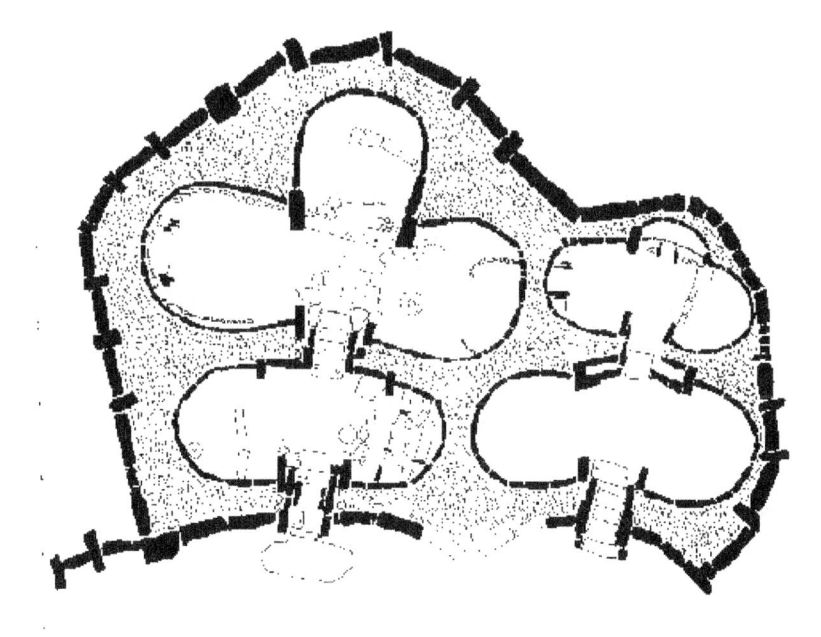

Plan of the Ġgantija Temples

The second temple at Ġgantija, to the north, was added around 400 to 500 years after the original south building, when part of the northern section of the boundary wall was removed to accommodate this extension, which, although smaller than the other, is quite similar in design apart from having an extremely small central niche.

Triple altar, left hand inner apse of the Southern temple

The internal fittings within both temples were fashioned out of the more workable Globigerina limestone, but they are quite scarce when compared with similar Maltese sites such as Ħaġar Qim and Tarxien. Apart from a few slabs here and there, some standing and some flat, most of the altars have disappeared into antiquity except a particularly fine triple table example, with dividing upright megaliths, on the rear wall of the left hand inner apse of the South Temple. These previously symmetrical trilithon structures now have modern pillars supporting the central and right hand horizontal slabs.

Another impressive altar nearly fills the right hand outer apse, also of the South Temple. Towards the rear wall this, unfortunately mainly ruined feature, includes ground level horizontal slabs with two flanking uprights. Two more higher uprights stand to either side, the left hand one with a significant curve carved into the inner edge and before these are two large blocks lying on the floor, across the entrance. These blocks are adorned with fine, if now faded, spiral carvings that can be made out more easily when wet or with the sunlight shining from the right direction. A further impressive carved block recovered from the South Temple was an upright pillar featuring a stylized snake down one of its narrow edges, a unique piece that can now be viewed in the Interpretation Centre. These embellished rocks, together with the pitted design to be found on some lower slabs, also in the South Temple, suggest that much more decorative carving would have been present when the temples were complete. A third area that has retained some of its fittings is the central niche area of the North Temple, where a horizontal slab, supported by three uprights, once filled the spread of the rear wall. Today the majority of this remains with only one section on the left part of this altar table missing.

Remains of altar, right hand outer apse of the South Temple

In modern times the Ġgantija Temples have been known about for hundreds of years and were regularly visited as part of the Grand Tour from the mid-17th century, when visitors would purchase paintings of the then called 'Giants Tower'. Tragically in 1827 Col. John Otto Bayer, the then Lieutenant Colonel of Gozo, had J. G. Vance of the Royal Engineers, conduct a clean-up of the site, which involved the removal of excess earth and rubble and it was during this operation that most of the ancient artefacts were lost and the site was then left abandoned. In 1933 the government took over ownership of the Ġgantija site and put it in the hands of the Museums

Department, who conducted numerous excavations over a sixty-year period from the time of acquisition.

Of the very few artefacts recovered from the actual temple site were two heads carved from Globigerina limestone, and many animal bones were located, as in other temples, suggesting animal sacrifice. There was evidence of fire residue in the temple although it is not clear whether cooking was taking place, as may have been the case in the large pots at Tarxien, or if this indicated the lightening of a dark building closed in and roofed by sealed timber beams. Fragments of plaster, two with traces of red ochre, were also found indicating that the temple walls, far from being rough and uneven had once been worked smooth and painted.

In 1949 a further haul of artefacts were found in a cave, probably an early rock-cut tomb, just 50 metres north of the temples, mainly consisting of broken offering bowls dating from the Ġgantija Period (3600 – 3200 BC), through to the Tarxien Period (3150 – 2500 BC). A small amount of human skulls and animal bones were also found mixed in with the pottery.

In more recent years the Ġgantija Temples became a UNESCO World Heritage Site in 1980 and extensive rehabilitation took place in the new millennium, work that has continued with the opening of the site as a heritage park in 2013.

The ancient temples of the Maltese islands are surely enigmatic and the mystery of how such a massive structure as the Ġgantija Temples were constructed on a small island like Gozo, with its limited resources appear to defy all reason. Evidence of settlements have been found around the Xagħra plateau and the large Xagħra Circle would account for burials, but this site in itself would appear extremely large for the size of the island. It is doubtful that the question as to whether Gozo could have supplied a large enough workforce with adequate logistics to complete this monumental building project will ever be answered.

Qala Menhir
(Il-Hagra L-Wieqfa – 'The Standing Stone')

Qala Menhir

The tiny town of Qala is just 3 km from the Mgarr ferry terminal, so finding the menhir named after it is a reasonably easy task. Taking the Triq ix-Xatt road up the hill from the port in the direction of Victoria, follow the sign, right and then right again towards Qala. On arriving on the edge of town take the left onto Triq It Tempju and having passed the school on the left, the monolith is hiding in its own strip of land, between the houses, on the right.

This gnarled old stone appears out of place in this built up area and it is far from clear whether it was meant to stand alone or if it was ever part on a larger site, maybe even a long disappeared temple. Single monoliths like this are rare on the Maltese islands although one can be found at the beginning of the Xemxija Trail, (covered below).

The nearby information plaque states that various Temple Period pottery shards and green-stone axe shaped pendants were found nearby and that the stone measures 2.7 meters at its widest and is a huge 3.9 meters in height. The sign also tells of the legend of a giantess, one and a half times taller than the stone. This massive woman, from Ta' Ċenċ, also on Gozo, where dolmens can be found (covered below), would sit on the stone spinning wool and munching on broad beans, this being the secret to her great strength.

Ta' Ċenċ Dolmen

Ta' Ċenċ Dolmen 1

The Ta' Ċenċ site is around 6.5 km from the Gozo ferry terminal and can be found by following signposts from Mgarr, through Xewkija and Sannat to the Ta' Ċenċ hotel. Helpfully there are also signs to the dolmen but having reached the hotel they are about 400 metres along the minor road that leads out into the open countryside, where the first dolmen is easily made out on the left.

The area here is quite barren but with extremely picturesque views across the island and out to sea over Comino to Malta in the distance. Dolmen 1, being the first site encountered stands out significantly as a man-made structure with a large capstone supported at four points by the seven small surrounding megalithic orthastats. It is not clear where the entrance would have been but the inner chamber is well defined, whilst any covering that may have once created a sealed mound, has long since disappeared.

Ta' Ċenċ Dolmen 2

The surrounding ground is of quite flat stone that appears to have smoothed out over many years of human activity suggesting that the area may have once been a large ceremonial place encompassing many more structures that can be seen today. Dolmen 2, is not in as good a state of repair as its nearby counterpart and its capstone has fallen completely on one side, whilst being supported by just two blocks to the other.

This is a fascinating site where the scattered stones stimulate the imagination and lend themselves to much interpretation. We will, of course, never know for sure what occurred here thousands of years ago in the Bronze Age, probably during the Tarxien Cemetery Period (2400 – 1500 BC), but when our ancestors selected this place for an important and probably holy place, it must have been, to some extent at least, for its aesthetic properties.

Xagħra Circle
(Brochtorff Circle)

Brochtorff's 1825 painting of the Xagħra Circle

On the island of Gozo, the Xagħra Circle is second in importance only to the magnificent Ġgantija Temples sitting on the Xagħra plateau only 400 metres away, a site that must have been built and used by the same ancient people. The circle, that was long known to the islanders, was dug out in the 1820s under the instructions of John Otto Bayer, the then Lieutenant Governor of Gozo. This work revealed a hollow in the ground containing a megalithic construction surrounded by a circular perimeter wall, 45 metres in diameter, consisting of megalithic stones lying closely together with, to the east, an entrance portal of two larger stones of around 4 metres in height which may have once supported a capstone to create a trilithon. The area was then re-covered and the surrounding stones eventually removed for new building works, but thankfully only after Charles Brochdorff had recorded the event in 1825/6 in watercolours and sketches and it is only in these artworks that any evidence of the original layout of the Xagħra Circle exists.

The site then lay forgotten until in 1964 Joseph Attard Tabone, a resident of the island, rediscovered its position by studying Brochdorff's works and fitting them into the landscape. This detective work enabled an excavation and major research project to be carried out jointly by the Malta Museums Department and the Universities of Malta and Cambridge between 1987 and 1994, headed by Dr Simon Stodart, Dr Caroline Malone and then Dr David Trump.

These extensive and lengthy excavations found pottery remains and a rock-cut tomb from the Żebbuġ Period (4100 – 3700 BC), suggesting that a human settlement was once present from that early time and that the surrounding ring of stones also dates from then.

A stone pavement is still present to some extent that would have led from the circle entrance, to the centre of the site and down some, long disappeared, steps into the burial chambers below. This central hollow was cleared of rubble to reveal an extensive series of natural, water formed, caves that had been extended and partitioned by carving into the hard Coralline limestone, a rock which does not easily lend itself to decorative fashioning.

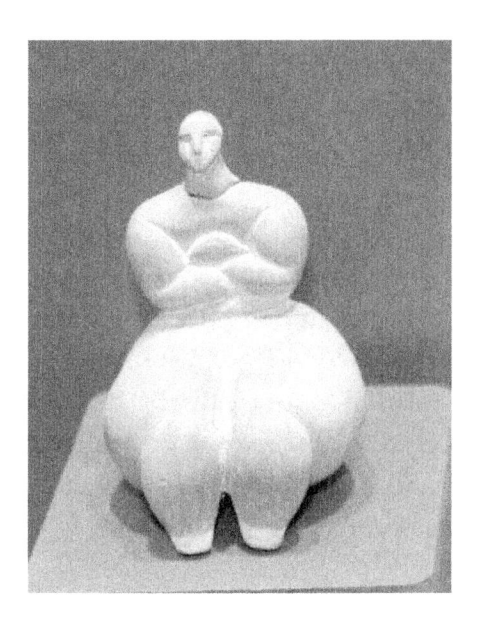

Fat Lady statue from the Xagħra Circle

The resulting space was far less ornate than the Ħal Saflieni Hypogeum, a structure of similar type. It is probably for this reason that a collection of trilithon altars and a large bowl of the more easily worked Globigerina limestone, moved to the site from nearby, were installed in the Tarxien Period (3150 – 2500 BC) to form a ritual area.

Malta & Gozo - A Megalithic Journey

figurine with triangular body from the Xagħra Circle

Work continues at the Xagħra Circle but the bones of over 1,000 humans have already been recovered, mainly separated into areas of long bones and skulls etc, although two complete male skeletons have been uncovered. These remains were found to be of a healthy population that must have enjoyed a good diet. The walls of one of the chambers showed traces of red ochre, a substance that has been long associated with ancient burials on the Maltese islands. Various artefacts were discovered near and amongst the bones such as small heads carved from bone and stone axe pendants, statues of the so called fat lady were also present as were some unusual figurines with triangular bodies. The majority of these finds are now on display at the Interpretation Centre at the Ġgantija Temples.

Epilogue

So this brings our journey around the magnificent Maltese islands and through the millennia to a completion, but whilst the Mediterranean sun still shines and the mysteries that surround these fascinating islands remain to tease the imagination the adventure will continue.

Will we ever know whether Palaeolithic man reached the islands? Will we ever find out who built the ancient temples? Will we ever be sure of when they were built, either in the Neolithic or well before? Why did these ingenious stone builders suddenly desert the islands? Whilst these and other questions still remain and whilst there are amazing ancient and historical sites to explore and discover I will be frequently visiting Malta and Gozo and running regular tours to the islands.

Humankind has been walking these islands for thousands of years – what a privilege to continue their legacy and to walk in their footsteps.

Bibliography

Attard, Joseph, Britain and Malta, The Story of an Era, Publishers Enterprises Group, 1995.

Attard, Joseph, The Knights of Malta, BDL Publishing, 1992.

Bible Society, Good News Bible, Collins Fount 1976

Blouet, Brian, The Story of Malta, Progress Press, 1989.

Bonanno, Anthony, Malta Phoenician, Punic and Roman, Midsea Books, 2005.

Bradford, Ernie, The Great Siege: 1565, Wordworth Edition, 1999.

Brincat, Joseph, M. Malta 870–1054. Al-Himyari's account and its linguistic implications, Said International, 1995.

Burgtorf, Jochen, The Central Convent of Hospitallers and Templars: history, organisation & personnel (1099/1129-1310), Brill, 2008

Cefai, Shirley. Cassar, Joann & Locatelli, Davide, San Pawl Milqi, Burmarrad, Malta – Presentation of a multi-cultural site in a changing landscape, University of Malta,

Camilleri, Fr Victor, Saint Agatha, Missionary Society of St Paul, 2001

Cardona, David, *Tas-Silg, From prehistoric temple to Byzantine church*, World Achaeology Magazine 59, 2013

Cardona, Neville & Depasquale, *The Domvs Romana*, Heritage Books, 2005

Caruana, Daphne, *Ġgantija Temples and Heritage Park*. Heritage Books, 2015

Castillo, Dennis Angelo, *The Maltese Cross: A Strategic History of Malta*, Praeger, 2005

Dalli, Charles, *Malta, The, Medieval Millennium*, Midsea Books, 2006

Davies, Norman, *Europe A History*, Pimlico, 1997

Freller, Thomas & Cilia, Daniel, *Malta, The Order of St John*, Midsea Books, 2010

Fabri, Nadia, *Ghar Dalam, The Cave, The Museum and the Garden*, Heritage Books, 2007.

Galea, Michael, *Malta Diary of War 1940-1945*, Publishers Enterprises Group Ltd, 1992

Garcia-Castellanos, Daniel, *Catastrophic flood of the Mediterranean after the Messinian salinity crisis*, Nature (journal) Vol 462, Pg 778, Dec 2009.

Giorgio, Cynthia de, *St John's Co-Cathedral*, Heritage Books 2007

Hancock, Graham, *Underworld*, Penguin Books, 2002

Malaterra, Geoffrey, *The Deeds of Count Roger of Calabria & Sicily & of Duke Robert Guiscard his brother* (translated by Graham A. Loud), 2005.

Malta Express, *Blackwood's Magazine*, February, 1980.

Mifsud, Anton & Mifsud, Simon, Dossier Malta, *Evidence for the Magdalenian*, Proprint Company, 1997

National Statistics Office, Malta, *Census of Population and Housing 2011, Preliminary Report*, National Statistics Office, Malta, 2012

Pace, Anthony, *The Hal Saflieni Hypogeum*, Heritage Books, 2004.

Pace, Anthony, *The Tarxien Temples*, Heritage Books, 2010.

Rudolf, Uwe Jens, & Berg, Warren, *Historical Dictionary of Malta*, Scarecrow Press, 2010.

Runciman, Steven, *Sicilian Vespers: A History of the Mediterranean World in the Later Thirteenth Century*, Cambridge University Press; Reprint edition (July 31, 1992)

Stroud Katya, *Hagar Qim & Mnajdra Prehistoric Temples*, Heritage Books, 2010.

Sultana, Sharon, *The National Museum of Archaeology*, Heritage Books, 2010.

Trump, H, David, *Cart-Ruts and their impact on the Maltese Landscape,* Heritage Books, 2008.

Trump, David & Cilia, Daniel, *Malta Prehistory and Temples,* Midsea Books, 2002.

Trump, H. David, *Malta: An Archaeological Guide,* Progress Press Co. Ltd. 1990.

Thackeray, William Makepeace, *Notes on a Journey from Cornhill to Grand Cairo,* Kessinger Publishing, 2010

Vella, Nicholas, C. *The Prehistoric Temples at Kordin III,* Heritage Books, 2004.

Wragg, David, *Malta, The Last Great Siege 1940-1943,* Leo Cooper, 2003

Professor Mario Buhagiar, *Malta's archaeology and ancient history: from the Bronze Age to the Byzantine*

Appendix
Sites by Time Period

The Neolithic Age
Ghar Dalam Cave
Borg in-Nadur

Temple Period
Hagar Qim Temples
Mnajdra Temples
Skorba Temple
Ta'Hagrat Temple
Tal-Qala Temple
Bugibba Hotel Temple
Ggantija
Tarxien Temples
Hal Saflieni Hypogeum
Kordin I & II
Kordin III
Tas-Silg Temple
Xemxija Rock cut caves and tombs
Qala Menhir
Xaghra Stone Circle

Bronze Age & Iron Age
Borg In-Nadur
Tarxien Cemetery
Wied Filep
Wied Zunber Dolmen
Ta'Hammut
Misqa Tanks
Birzebbuga Silos & Cisterns
Clapham Junction & Catacomb Caves
Ta'Cenc

Roman
Domus Romana
St Paul Milqi
Catacombs of St. Paul

Knights of St John
City of Valletta
St. John's Co-Cathedral
Governor's Palace & Armory
The Three Cities
Coastal Fortifications

The British
Victoria Lines
Mosta Church & Dome

Other Books by Neil McDonald

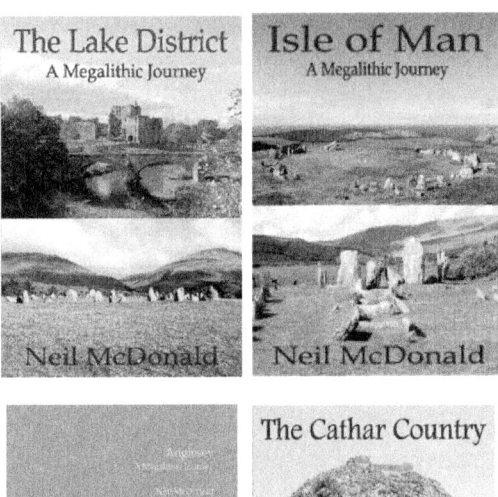

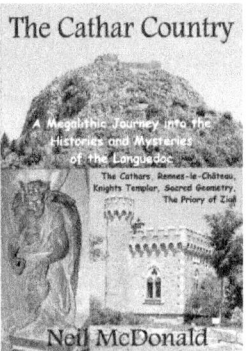

The Lake District, A Megalithic Journey
Isle of Man, A Megalithic Journey
Anglesey, A Megalithic Journey
The Cathar Country, A Megalithic Journey

Available from
www.megalithictours.com

Malta & Gozo - A Megalithic Journey

Neil McDonald runs 'Megalithic Tours', to ancient, mystical and historical sites around Britain, France, Portugal and Malta; from the famous Stonehenge, where we have private access, Callanish in the Outer Hebrides, Orkney and Shetland the amazing stone alignments of Carnac in Northern France etc; to many little known, hidden gems. The Megalithic Tours website contains an up to date timetable.

Megalithic Tours

50 Cottam Avenue
Ingol, Preston,
Lancashire
PR2 3XH. UK

01772 728181 – 07799 061991
neil@mysteriousearthclub.com

www.megalithictours.com

Printed in Great Britain
by Amazon